Miss Dahl's
voluptuous
delights

Miss Dahl's voluptuous delights

Recipes for Every Season, Mood and Appetite

photographs by Jan Baldwin

WILLIAM MORROW
An Imprint of HarperCollinsPublishers

For Jamie, at whose table I wish
to grow old. With all my love.

This book was first published in Great Britain in 2009 by HarperCollins,
an imprint of HarperCollins Publishers Ltd.

HarperCollins books may be purchased for educational, business,
or sales promotional use. For information please write:
Special Markets Department, HarperCollins Publishers,
10 East 53rd Street, New York, NY 10022.

FIRST EDITION

Design by Patrick Budge
Photographs by Jan Baldwin
Stylist: Susie Theodorou

Library of Congress Cataloging-in-Publication Data has been applied for.

ISBN 978-0-06-145099-0

10 11 12 13 14   RRD   10 9 8 7 6 5 4 3 2

contents

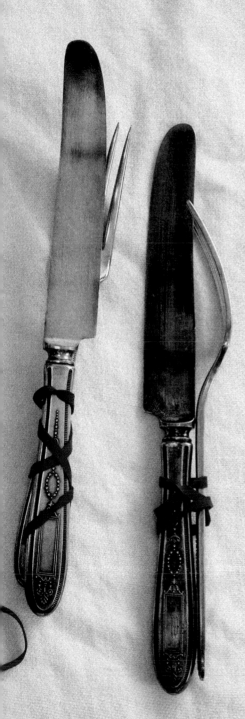

Cook's Notes	vi
Introduction	viii
Autumn	1
Breakfasts	17
Lunches	33
Suppers	51
Winter	67
Breakfasts	81
Lunches	95
Suppers	109
Spring	129
Breakfasts	147
Lunches	161
Suppers	175
Summer	193
Breakfasts	203
Lunches	217
Suppers	231
Desserts	243
Acknowledgments	271
Index	273
Suppliers	276

cook's notes

All pepper is freshly ground black pepper. I also use good-quality sea salt, such as Maldon.

Eggs/dairy/stock/poultry: try to use organic, free-range where possible. If you are pregnant, avoid raw or lightly cooked eggs and unpasteurized cheeses. For stock I use either fresh or vegetable bouillon; Marigold Swiss Vegetable Bouillon Powder is very good.

Citrus fruit: if the zest is to be used, buy unwaxed citrus fruit.

Crème fraîche: American readers can substitute sour cream.

introduction

The second word I ever spoke was *crunch* – muddled baby speak for fudge, which should have alerted my parents to what lay ahead. As a small child, food occupied both my waking and nocturnal thoughts; I had clammy nightmares about dreadful men made from school mashed potato wearing striped tights, chasing me into dense forests.

A welcome dream was a cloud made of trifle, a slick spring bubbling with chocolate or a fountain bursting with forbidden Sprite or Cherry Coke. My dolls had the fanciest tea parties in London and I kept a tight guest list, so the only person actually benefiting from the tea was me. My first (and last) rabbit was named for my then favorite breakfast food, the pancake. Pancake was a brute, and he performed an unnatural sex act upon his hutchmate, Maple Syrup, who was a docile, blinking guinea pig. The shock killed Maple Syrup immediately and Pancake was banished to the country to live out the rest of his days in shame and isolation. It seemed unfair that his strange peccadilloes were rewarded with buxom country rabbits and fresh grass, but the karma police intervened and he met a gruesome end in the jaws of a withered fox.

I have always had a passionate relationship with food; passionate in that I loved it blindly or saw it as its own entity, rife with problems. Back in the day, in my esteem, food was either a faithful friend or a sin, rarely anything in between. Eating as sin is a concept more pertinent than ever before in this tricky, unforgiving today. I realized at an early age that I was born in the wrong time, foodwise. I would have been infinitely more suited to the court of Henry VIII, where the burgeoning interest I showed in food would have been encouraged and celebrated. Alas, in my London of the eighties it was simply cause for family mirth, sullen trips to the nutritionist and brown rice diets. Oddly enough, I was reasonably skinny with a great round moon face; just perpetually hungry like a baby bird. I got rather chubby and unfortunate-looking when I was about seven, and there are some rather sinister pictures of me looking like a grumpy old woman (I had a penchant for coral lipstick and any church-type hat), always with a large sandwich hanging out of my mouth.

I grew up surrounded by food lovers; my parents, Tessa and Julian, were natural cooks and both sets of grandparents were known for a full table. My earliest memories of food involve my paternal grandmother, Gee-Gee (an ex chorus-girl dancer, five feet of endless leg, saucer-blue eyes and marcelled blond waves), who lived on the Sussex coast in a house surrounded by whispering trees. My dad and I would drive down from London, a journey that felt decades long to a child, but the monotony was forgotten as soon as Gee-Gee swung open the front door and we were embraced; first by a pleasurable blast of something roasting, and then by her. These lunches usually incorporated roasted something with gravy, Yorkshire pudding, roast potatoes, parsnips, cauliflower cheese, and definitely dessert: treacle tart with a cool lick of cream to sophisticate and sharpen the sugar; incredible crumbles, swimming in thick vanilla custard. Every day there was proper tea at Gee-Gee's, with homemade scones, ginger cake and her best bone-thin china. She understood absolutely everything about life, except three things:

1. Why anyone, most specifically me, would become a vegetarian.
2. Why it was difficult for hunger to be limited to three times a day, with a little pang left over for tea, devoid of desire to pick between meals.
3. The attraction of violently colored eye shadow to a sixteen-year-old. ("Like an ancient barmaid," she'd sniff at my peacock-feather-green eyelids.)

Gee-Gee was brilliant; she taught me to bake without fuss. I watched the quiet joy she derived from feeding those she loved and I took it with me like a tattoo into adulthood, making idle breakfasts and Sunday lunches, Indian summer dinners and rainy day teas, revelling in the simple pleasure of cooking for people I cared about brought me.

If anything, this book is a total homage to my family and the appetite and culinary legacy they left me with: Gee-Gee; my maternal grandmother, Patricia, of Knoxville, Tennessee, with her fondness for grits, collard greens and lemon chiffon pie; my Norwegian grandfather, Roald, and his vast appreciation for chocolate, borscht and burgundy; his second wife, Felicity, who in his absence continues to keep his table with the same spirit and standard; my aunts and uncle, fine cooks all; my mum and dad, my brothers and sister. Each and every one of them has an influence in here somewhere.

I am not an authority on anything much, but I do feel qualified to talk about eating. I've done a lot of it. In my time I have been both round as a Rubens and a little slip-shadow of a creature. Weight, and the "how-to" maintenance of it, seems to be something that preoccupies a lot of people, and because I lost some, rather publicly, it is something people feel free to ask me about. I have had conversations about weight with strangers in supermarkets, on airplanes and in bathroom queues. I could talk until the cows come home about food and recipes and bodies and why as people we are so consumed by the three. I have sat next to erudite academic types at dinner, steeling myself for a conversation that will doubtless include something I know nothing about, like physics, only to be asked in a surreptitious tone, "How did you get thinner?" At which stage I will laugh and say, "Well, it all started like this . . ."

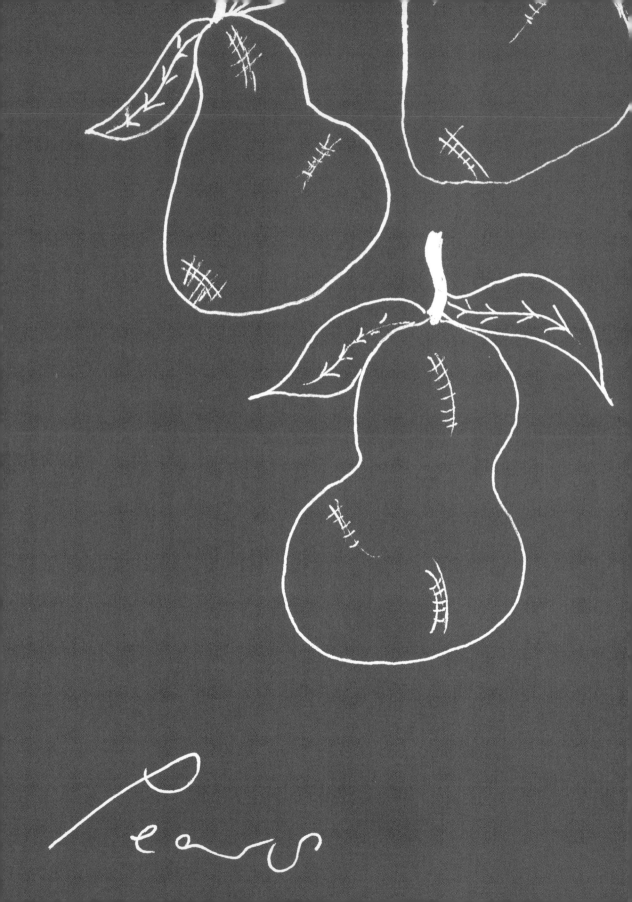

Pears

autumn

BREAKFASTS

Poached eggs on portobello mushrooms with goat's cheese
Rice pudding with pear purée
Omelette with caramelized red onion and Red Leicester
Tawny granola
Musician's breakfast (homemade bread with Parma ham)
Indian sweet potato pancakes
Baked haddock ramekin

LUNCHES

Spinach and watercress salad with goat's cheese
French onion soup
Squid salad with char-grilled peppers and
    cilantro dressing
Baked eggs with Swiss chard
Chicken and halloumi kebabs with chanterelles
Spinach barley soup
Buckwheat risotto with wild mushrooms

SUPPERS

Peasant soup
Sunday roast chicken and trimmings
Paris mash
Sea bass in tarragon and wild mushroom sauce
Lily's stir-fry with tofu
Eggplant Parmigiana
Grilled salmon with baked onions

We begin in the autumn because that's when everything changed. Autumn is a season I love more than any other; for its smoky sense of purpose and half-lit mornings, its bonfires, baked potatoes, nostalgia, chestnuts and Catherine wheels.

It was late September. I was eighteen. I had experienced a rather unceremonious exit from school. I had no real idea about what I wanted to do, just some vague fantasies involving writing, a palazzo, an adoring Italian, daily love letters and me in a Sophia Loren sort of dress, weaving through a Roman market holding a basket of ripe scented figs. I had just tried to explain this to my mother over lunch at a restaurant on Elizabeth Street in London. She was not, curiously, sharing my enthusiasm.

"Enough," she said. "No more alleged history of art courses. You're going to secretarial college to learn something useful, like typing."

"But I need to learn about culture!" She gave me a very beady look.

"That's it," she said. "No more. End of conversation."

"But I . . ." The look blackened. I resorted to the historic old faithful between teenagers and their mothers.

"God . . . Why don't you understand? None of you understand me!"

I ran out into the still, grey street, sobbing. I threw myself on a doorstep and lit a bitter cigarette. And then something between serendipity and Alice in Wonderland magic happened.

A black taxi chugged to a halt by the doorstep on which I sat. Out of it fell a creature that surpassed my Italian imaginings. She wore a ship on her head, a miniature galleon with proud sails that billowed in the wind. Her white bosom swelled out of an implausibly tiny corset and she navigated the street in neat steps, teetering on the brink of five-inch heels.

Her arms were full to bursting with hatboxes and carrier bags and she was alternately swearing, tipping the taxi driver and honking a great big laugh. I remember thinking: "I don't know who that is, but I want to be her friend." I was so fascinated I forgot to cry.

I stood up and said, "Do you need any help with your bags?"

"Oh yes!" she said. "Actually, you *are* sitting on my doorstep.

"So, why were you crying?" The ship woman said in her bright pink kitchen. It transpired that she was called Isabella Blow; she was contributing editor at *Vogue* and something of a fashion maverick. We'd put the bags down and she was making tea in a proper teapot.

"I was crying about my *future*," I said heavily. "My mother doesn't understand me. I don't know what I'll do. Oh, it's so awful."

"Oh, don't worry about that. Pfff!" she said. "Do you want to be a model?"

If it had been a film, there would have been the audible ting of a fairy wand. I looked at her incredulously. "Yes," I said, thinking of avoiding the purdah of shorthand. My next question was, "Are you sure?"

The "Are you sure?" didn't spring from some sly sense of modesty; it was brutal realism. And not of the usual model standard "I was such an ugly duckling at school, and everyone teased me about how painfully skinny I was" kind.

Bar my height, I couldn't have looked any less like a model. I had enormous tits, an even bigger arse and a perfectly round face with plump, smiling cheeks. The only thing I could have possibly shared with a model was my twisted predilection for chain smoking.

But for sweet Issy, as I came to know her, none of this posed a problem. She saw people as she chose to see them; as grander cinematic versions of themselves.

"I think," she said, her red lips a post-box stamp of approval, "I think you're like Anita Ekberg." I pretended I knew whom she was talking about.

"Ah yes. Anita Ekberg." I said.

"Now put on some lipstick and we'll go and find your mother and tell her we've found you a career."

We celebrated our fortuitous meeting, with my now mollified

"Now put on some lipstick and we'll tell your mother we've found you a career"

mother in tow, at a Japanese restaurant in Mayfair, toasting my possible new career with a wealth of sushi and tempura.

"Gosh, you *do* like to eat," Issy said, eyes wide, watching as my chopsticks danced over the plates. I would have said yes but my mouth was full.

Social activities in England often revolve around the tradition of the nursery tea. I was deeply keen on tea, but as an only child I was *not* at all keen on having to share either my toys or my food.

"You must learn to share. It's a very nasty habit, selfishness," Maureen, my Scottish nanny, said, her grey eyes fixed on me in a penetrating way.

"Urgh. It's so unfair!" I would cry, scandalized by the injustice of having to watch impotent as other children, often strangers, were allowed to torture my dolls and eat all the salt and vinegar crisps for the mere reason that "they can do what they want – they are your guests."

But I didn't invite them! You did. I don't want them messing up my dressing-up box and smearing greasy fingers on my best one-eyed doll, or asking to see her "front bottom." I don't want friends who say "front bottom." I want to play Tarzan and Jane with Dominic from next door, who has brown eyes and kissed me by the compost heap. I don't want to be the ugly stepsister in the game, I want to be Cinderella! No, I'm not tired. I might go to my room now and listen to *Storyteller*. They can stay in the playroom on their own.

When I was six, my friend Ka-Ming came for tea. There was macaroni and cheese, and for dessert, yogurt. Maureen announced in her buttery burr that there were only two yogurts, chocolate and strawberry, on which Ka-Ming, as the guest, got first dibs. Agonizing as Ka-Ming slowly weighed the boons of each flavor, I excused myself and ran to the playroom, where the wishing stone my grandmother Gee-Gee had found on the beach sat on the bookshelf. I had one wish left.

"Please, wishing stone and God, let her not pick the chocolate yogurt, because that is the one I want." I cradled the stone, hot in my palm.

I walked into the kitchen to find Ka-Ming already eating the strawberry yogurt with enthusiasm. The chocolate Mr.

Men yogurt sat sublime on my plate. This turn of fate cemented my belief that if you wish for something hard enough, as long as it doesn't already belong to somebody else you tend to get it.

At ten, to my great dismay, I was sent to boarding school. I recalled the permanent midnight feasts in Enid Blyton books, and reckoned that this was the sole pro in an otherwise dismal situation. Yet on arrival I realized that the halcyon midnight feasts were a myth. The reality was fried bread swimming in its own stagnant grease, powdered mashed potatoes, bright pink ham, gristly stew, grey Scotch eggs and collapsed beets, which I was made to eat in staggering quantity.

The consolation prize when home from boarding school was picking a Last Supper. Last Suppers were cooked the final night of the school holidays by my mother at her bottle-green Aga; a balm to the palate before another term of unspeakably horrible food. I chose these suppers as if I were dining at the captain's table on the *Titanic* – beef consommé, roast chicken wrapped in bacon with tarragon creeping wistfully over its breast, potatoes golden and gloriously crispy on the outside and flaking softly within, and peas buttered and sweet, haloed by mint from the garden. Desserts were towering, trembling creations: lemon mousse, scented with summer; chocolate soufflés, bitter and proud.

We were grumpily ambivalent about the food at school; the English as a rule aren't a race of protesters, particularly the ten-year-olds. School food was meant to be bad; that was its role before the advent of Jamie Oliver and his luscious organic, sustainable school dinners. There was the merest whiff of protest during the salmonella crisis in the late eighties, when some rebel chalked "Eggwina salmonella curry" over the curried eggs listed on the menu board and got a detention for her efforts, but that was about as racy as it ever got.

I left boarding school at twelve, and we moved from starchy London to svelte New York. It was in this year that food first became something other than what you ate of necessity, boredom or greediness. I noticed that food contained its own brand of inherent *power*, certainly where adults were concerned. Women in New York talked about food and how to avoid it all the time. Their teenage progeny religiously counted fat grams, while the mothers went to see a tanned diet guru named Dr. R, who provided neat white pills and Ziploc bags for snacks of mini pretzels, asking them out for fastidious dinners, where he monitored their calorie consumption. If they were lucky they might get a slimline kiss at the end of the evening, the bow of his leonine head offering dietary benediction. It was a savvy way of doing business; Dr. R had a repeat clientele, as all the divorced mums were in love with him, staying five pounds over their ideal weight in order to prolong both that coveted dinner and his undivided attention.

I loved New York, loved its fast glittery shininess and sophistication, which was the polar opposite of the dowdy certainty of English boarding school. At my new school, my ineptitude with math was greeted with such bolstering and enthusiasm that, for a brief blissful period, I was almost good at it.

In our biology class we read about the perils of anorexia. We learned the signs to be wary of: secrecy, layers of clothing, blue extremities, pretending to have eaten earlier, cessation of menstruation, hair on the body, compulsive exercise.

We were eagle-eyed mini detectives, each classmate a suspect. After these sessions we didn't see the irony in spending the whole of lunchtime talking about how many calories were in a plain bagel and who looked fat in her leotard. Awareness of eating disorders seemed American-specific; my friends in England were baffled by it.

"Isn't Anna Rexia a person?" My best friend asked me on a crackling transatlantic line.

"Duh," I said.

There was a pause.

"That's really awful. Why would anyone not want to eat when they were hungry?"

Cafeteria food in America was even worse than in England; gloopy electric-orange macaroni and cheese, iron-tasting chocolate milk and "pudding," a gelatinous mess meant to be related to vanilla in some way. I stuck to whole wheat bagels with cream cheese and tomatoes, because that was low-fat,

My taste buds awoke from their slumber with the tenacity of Rip Van Winkle

and the then wisdom told us that low-fat was the way forward. On a Friday morning we were allowed to bring breakfast to school and eat it in our first class as a treat. I bought these breakfasts from the deli on the corner and did consider them treats; a fried egg sandwiched in a croissant and milky coffee (made with skimmed milk, of course) seemed deliciously adult and forbidden.

I shaved my legs for the first time at thirteen without permission and left ribbons of skin in the bath with my shaky novice hand. My mother came in and shook her head and said sadly, "Now you've started there's no going back. That'll be waxing for the rest of your life, my darling."

I wondered how I might look to other people in a swim-suit, as during the summer there were pool parties where there were boys, and, perhaps even more scary, the narrow eyes of the other girls. It seemed much more complicated territory than my English boarding school, where everyone was blue from cold, clad in the same troll-like, unflattering regulation green. These golden girls wore tiny bikinis and had manicures and pedicures.

In the absence of hearty boarding school stodge and endless picking, my body had willowed. My legs were long; my skirts were short. I was a wisp with a wasp waist and pertly chested to boot. I joined the chattering lunchtime throng, reading food labels as if they were Dostoyevsky, pretending to understand, while at home I tore up steps on the StairMaster as Jason Priestley twinkled at me from the television.

For reasons complicated and long, we left the sophisticated city when I was fourteen and fell heavily down to earth, onto England's sodden soil, in 1991. No one seemed to have heard of "low-fat" in England, not even in London where I was now at day school. They didn't seem to care all that much. I tried for a few gruelling months to avoid the fat in food I'd learned to be careful of, but it just kept coming back, persistent as a lover spurned.

I eventually surrendered on a half-term holiday in France with school friends who were eating their croissants and drinking their full-fat milk hot chocolate with deep abandon. Having ascertained that there really was no skimmed milk in the house (or indeed the country), I took the plunge. But oh!

How delicious! My taste buds awoke from their New York slumber with the tenacity of Rip Van Winkle and they never slept again.

My body responded, and how; my cheeks plumped up like an indolent Matisse lady's. On the street, my complicated curves and awkward wiggle sent a message that my brain and heart could not keep up with. Grown men called out to me; dark adult things in sly tones. I found this unsettling and felt naked even when I was dressed. Yet I dressed the part of the vixen in viciously heeled shoes, breasts jutting forward proudly, betrayed only by my eyes. I was constantly followed home from school, and flashed at on the bus. My mother despaired and sent me to a progressive boarding school in Hampshire, surrounded by fields, where I could stomp around in my inappropriate clothing without being accosted by potential rapists. We lived on bread, and I filled myself brimful with it; warm and soft from the local bakery, covered in butter and Marmite.

Because of my school's nice progressive nature, there was an abundance of personal choice and options. I discovered one could opt out of games and do something called "Outdoor Work," so I opted out and tottered off to the woods in my suede miniskirts, lamely clutching a saw as I pretended to erect fences with the boys who still played Dungeons & Dragons. Our fences were spindly, rickety efforts and our pig-tending was not much better.

On Wednesday we had a half-day of school to make up for the fact that we had school on Saturday and we were allowed to go into the nearby town in the afternoons, as long as we stayed clear of the pub. My interest in the pub was cursory. On Tuesday nights I planned epic gastronomic excursions, formulating the menu of what and where I would eat, the conclusion invariably involving an epic fiesta of cake and clotted cream.

Unsurprisingly, at boarding school I gained two stone (nearly thirty pounds). It happened quite by accident, and I didn't even notice to begin with, but you can't exist on bread and cake, with your sole exercise taking the form of watching other people build things, and stay thin. It didn't occur to me how I could have contributed, or that I could do anything about any of it.

I just thought it was yet another adolescent unfairness foisted upon me. I ate more cake, read tragic French novels and hated the fields and stupid fences I was surrounded by. I longed for London, a minor Parisian appetite, lithe limbs, complication and Chantal Thomas knickers. Mercifully, the knowledge of how to acquire such things remained totally out of my reach.

My country sojourn over, I arrived back in London at sixteen with child-bearing hips and a trunk full of smocks. Everyone pretended not to notice. Sixth form was in Golders Green, and instead of café dining once a week on a Wednesday, planning lunch in the local establishments became a blissful daily affair. This is where all of my summer babysitting money went. At the bottom of Golders Hill, near the station, there was an amazing kosher deli where I ordered fresh bagels, sweet and doughy inside, smothered with thick cream cheese and smoked salmon. In Golders Hill Park, it was the sweet little Italian café where you could get a plate of *al dente* penne with a smoky tomato sauce and dear little cream-filled pastries for dessert. The pub at the top of the hill was all about jacket potatoes and a fine ploughman's. But what jacket potatoes – twice-baked and filled with butter, Gruyère and watercress, or the alternative: tuna, mayonnaise and sweet corn. I think I tried to go on a diet once, and it involved, from what I can remember, eating a lot of brown rice and apples and lecithin, because a friend of my mother's told me that they all lived on it in the seventies and that it melted fat clean away. In the sixth form games were no longer compulsory, and I began to feel the same way about school, causing an academic rift that I rue to this day.

Between school and modelling, before I met Isabella, I was first a nanny, then a waitress. Both were perilous where food was concerned. As a nanny, I was constantly picking at left-over fish fingers, Twiglets, egg sandwiches and Victoria sponge. The two girls I looked after were incredibly sweet: a round baby and a six-year-old with a voice like Marianne Faithfull. We went to lots of rather posh tea parties where the mothers greeted me as "Nanny." I adored the little girls but was a bit hopeless really; not ironing their clothes, taking naps with them and trying on their mother's scent when she was

I tottered off to the woods, lamely clutching a saw

out. I was very much eighteen. We did, however, make each other laugh, and I loved Jaffa cakes as much as they did.

And not for me the kind of waitressing job where I ran on skinny legs around a steamy frantic environment, collapsing at the end of a twelve-hour shift in sheer anemic exhaustion. No, I went to work the 7:00 a.m. shift in a coffee-shop bakery after the baking had already taken place. Thus, my arrival coincided happily with things coming out of the oven: a muffin with apple butter, a dark molasses banana bread. I think it was my all-time favorite job. It involved chatting, smiling, eating and concocting lovely coffee-based milkshakes which I would sip through the day. I was an awful waitress, because I was clumsy and could never remember anyone's order. But they were terribly sweet there, and I learned how to sweep a floor properly, and that you cannot wear five-inch peep-toed mules to waitress in.

When I began modelling after those brief jobs, I was completely unprepared for the onslaught of curiosity it carried with it. I was in that funny teenage place of being both very aware of, and yet somehow forgetting I had a body. I wanted to look the same as my friends; I wanted to be able to borrow their clothes. Beyond that, I didn't think about it too deeply.

I was dripping in diamonds and not a great deal else

Issy had never told me to lose weight; she had just said rather vaguely, "Now, my love; no more chips and puddings for you, and always wear a good bra and red lipstick." My concession to this advice was a DIY diet: eating instant powdered soup with dry pita bread for three days, which was revolting, and certainly had no effect. I ended up being measured for a bra at Rigby and Peller, which had an infinitely more tangible result than the soup, and also developed a lifelong love affair with Yves Saint Laurent's Rouge Pur, which smells of roses.

It was Issy who introduced me to Sarah Doukas, the founder of Storm Model Management, and when she signed me, weight loss was nowhere on the day's agenda. Sarah is famously visionary; she discovered Kate Moss at JFK airport when she was fourteen and manages her to this day. With her customary canniness, she saw that there might actually be a place for me in fashion, given the vocal protest the media were making against the so-called "heroin chic" look that was defining style. The timing and her instinct made a happy marriage to set the scene for what was about to happen.

My first job was being photographed nude by Nick Knight for *ID* magazine. They gave me five-inch long silver nails, silver contact lenses and a canvas of skin powdered silver. I don't remember feeling naked; I felt like an onlooker, such was the transformative power of the hair and makeup, which took four hours. The overriding memory I have of that day is of being turned into someone else; some alter ego with comic-book curves and a rapacious smile. Being naked seemed almost incidental. A few hours later I was sent in a cab up to Park Royal to be shot by David La Chapelle for *Vanity Fair* in a portfolio about "Swinging London," this time clad in a string bikini. When I went home late that night, I didn't wash my makeup off because I wanted to wake up looking like that forever. Of course the next morning I was a smeared shell of a creature, my sheets covered in silver dust.

A few weeks later, I boarded a train to Paris, carrying nothing but a little basket with my nightdress, knickers and a toothbrush, and went straight from the Gare du Nord to the house of Karl Lagerfeld, who was shooting a story for German *Vogue* about King Farouk. Gianfranco Ferré was playing the part of the erstwhile king, and I his bawdy American mistress. I was dripping in diamonds and not a great deal else. I felt incredibly shy around Mr. Lagerfeld, who was kind yet reticent behind his fan, until he roared with laughter, pinched my cheeks and kissed me like an uncle. We stopped for a proper French lunch, a stew heavy with red wine, oozing cheese and crusty bread and little pots of dense, dark chocolate for dessert. I was in heaven. The shoot went on long into the night, and after everyone else had gone home he photographed me waltzing around his beautiful library, which shone with swathes of waxy lilies and hundreds of candles. At 3:00 a.m. I walked across the street to the old-fashioned hotel where I was staying, and I lay in bed with my eyes wide open, unable to summon sleep. There was so much to absorb and evoke, from the books that lined the walls from floor to ceiling, to the churchlike smell of the lilies, the cool of the diamonds as they slipped around my neck, the food . . .

People had noticed me. Big women from all over the world wrote me congratulatory letters, commending my big bold form. Morning television shows wanted to interview me. Newspapers breathlessly reported my strange fleshy phenomena; a welcome backlash, finally, against the x-ray fashion industry. In the wake of the very angular, it seemed people wanted an anti-waif; a sensual woman who indulged in whatever she wanted, whenever she wanted it. By default, this became me. But reflection on what it represented and what it might mean had escaped me; no longer reliant on waitress's wages, I was too busy skipping around London, Paris, New York and Milan, spending my modelling money in posh restaurants, city appropriate. I went to Nobu for the first time and nearly died with pleasure – that black cod! In Italy it was risotto, in Paris remoulade, and New York was just a culinary world mecca, full stop.

I remember doing shows in the early days, happily squeezed into some mini little thing. Although a walk up and down a runway is over in minutes, you can register the faces of those you walk by in slow motion. I produced such a strange mixed reaction, one that was palpable. The more formidable fashion editors would sit there with their arms tightly crossed, looking embarrassed and rolling their eyes. Others would cheer and shout. The photographers at the end of the runway would sometimes catcall and whistle. It had been a long time since the advent of tits in fashion, so they were pretty enthused. I found a sort of sad teenage validation in this – not particularly thought out or examined – something along the lines of "It's men, whistling at me. They seem to fancy me. Hurrah! That must mean I'm kind of sexy."

Every woman in my family had been through a tricky adolescent over-spilling phase. The difference with mine was that it became both representative and a matter of public record, rather than something to look back on with tender mirth when presented with a family album. We always joked as a family about our greediness. We described events by what we ate. There was, and is, a total ease and pleasure around food and cooking. My path has been a funny one, having come from such a background, to then find myself at a formative age dropped into the middle of an industry not exactly renowned for its epicurean appreciation. There's something sort of fun and subversive about it. It was a slightly wiggly trajectory, but one full of interesting stuff.

And guess what? I'm now right back where I was at seven, minus the penchant for coral lipstick and bad hats. I just couldn't get away from the siren call of the kitchen that is an inherent part of me. The kitchen of which I speak is both literal and metaphoric. It's the sum of what I've learned so far, and am still learning.

This kitchen is a gentle relaxed one, where a punishing, guilt-inducing attitude towards food will not be tolerated. In this kitchen we appreciate the restorative powers of chocolate. The kitchen would have a fireplace, and possibly a few dogs from Battersea Dogs' Home curled up next to it. There might be a small upright piano by the window, with an orchid that doesn't wither as soon as I look at it. On long summer days, the doors to this kitchen are thrown open, while a few lazy, nonstinging bees mosey by. Children stir. When it rains, there is room in this kitchen for reading and a spoon finding its way into the cake mix. Serious cups of tea are drunk here; idle gossip occurs, balance and humor prevail. It's the kitchen of my grandparents, but with some Bowie thrown in. It is lingering breakfasts, it is friends with babies on their knees, it is good-bye on a Sunday with the promise of more. This kitchen is where life occurs; jumbled, messy and delicious.

It is lovely.

There is room in this kitchen for a spoon finding its way into the cake mix

autumn
breakfasts

Poached eggs on portobello mushrooms with goat's cheese

SERVES 2

2 generously sized
  portobello
  mushrooms
Salt and pepper
Olive oil
2 thick rounds of soft
  goat's cheese
2 eggs
1 teaspoon of white
  vinegar (for
  poaching)
1 sprig of fresh
  tarragon, chopped

I make this when I'm a bit breaded out, but hungry. Portobello mushrooms have a satisfying meatiness about them that sates without the heaviness of a full English breakfast.

Preheat the broiler. Wash the mushrooms and remove the stems, season with salt and pepper and give them a glug of olive oil; a spoonful should do. Crumble the goat's cheese.

Pop the mushrooms stem side up under the broiler for about 5 minutes. While they are searing away, poach the eggs in a pan of gently boiling water (a teaspoon of white vinegar should stop them from separating).

You can do one of two things with the goat's cheese: you can add it on top of the mushrooms when you put them under the broiler, so it browns; or you can put it on just after they come out.

You should poach the eggs for about 3 minutes if you want them soft in the middle (5 if you want them stern and unyielding). Drain them, put them on top of your crumbly goat's cheese/mushroom mix, scatter some chopped tarragon on the top, grind on a bit of pepper and *voilà*!

Rice pudding with pear purée

There is a theme to my cooking that tends towards baby food. This is a perfect example.

In a heavy-bottomed pan, bring the milk and rice to the boil. Add the cardamom pods and cinnamon stick. Take the heat down to its lowest flame or use a heat diffuser, cover the rice, and simmer for 20 minutes, stirring occasionally.

While this is cooking, peel and core the pears and chop into slices. Bring the apple juice to the boil; add the pears and cinnamon. Cook until the pears are tender, 5 minutes or so, adding more juice if needed. Remove from the heat and transfer to a blender, or purée them with a handheld blender.

Fluff the rice and put into a bowl. Pour the compote on top with a drizzle of honey or maple syrup and, if it's a particularly grim morning, stick in a spoonful of crème fraîche.

SERVES 2

1½ cups of the milk of
    your choice – I'd use
    2% or soy
½ cup of basmati rice
2 cardamom pods,
    lightly crushed
1 stick of cinnamon
Honey or maple syrup,
    to taste
Crème fraîche
    (optional)

For the compote
2 pears
¼ cup of apple juice
1 teaspoon of
    cinnamon extract

Omelette with caramelized red onion and Red Leicester

SERVES 1
½ a small red onion
Olive oil
2 eggs
Salt and pepper
2oz of Red Leicester
  cheese (any good,
  sharp, hard Cheddar
  or a Monterey Jack
  will do as an
  alternative)

I cry like a baby when I chop onions. A few years ago I found a brilliant device from Williams-Sonoma online which does all the work for you. You simply peel the onion, put it in the top of the contraption, pop the lid on and turn the handle. *Voilà*, diced onions without tears.

Roughly chop the onion. On a low flame, heat 1 tablespoon of olive oil in a nonstick frying pan. I use a small fat pan as I like my omelettes tidy and plump. Gently fry the onion, letting the edges brown but making sure the middle stays softly purple. This should take about 5 minutes. When it looks to your liking, take it out and set aside. Remove any crispy bits from the pan.

Beat the eggs and season. On a low heat again, heat a scant bit of olive oil in your frying pan and add the eggs. Let them settle for 30 seconds. Either grate or break the cheese up into rough chunks and put it in the setting omelette. As it melts, pour in your onions and gently fold the omelette in half with a spatula. Depending on how done you like your omelette to be, you can then fry the other side. I like mine very slightly oozing.

Delicious with a dollop of mustard! (And if you are my persnickety brother, Ned, without the onions!)

Tawny granola

You can eat this with milk as a cereal, sprinkle it on yogurt or porridge or simply stick your paw in the jar throughout the day. It makes one feel very fifties housewife, because as it bakes the house is bathed in a warm cinnamony glow.

Preheat the oven to 350°F and oil a large rimmed cookie sheet.

In a mixing bowl combine the oats, pumpkin seeds, almonds and coconut. In a separate large mixing bowl, mix all of the wet ingredients and the spices. Combine the dry ingredients into the wet.

Spread the mixture out evenly on the cookie sheet, using a spatula to smooth it down. Bake for around 40 minutes, keeping an eye on the granola. When it starts to brown, turn the mixture over with the spatula to make sure it toasts evenly on both sides.

When it is ready, take it out of the oven, let it cool, then add the apricots.

Store in an airtight container and serve with milk or yogurt, or eat as a snack when the whim takes you.

SERVES 4–6

Oil for greasing
2 cups of rolled oats
½ cup of pumpkin seeds
½ cup of sliced almonds
½ cup of unsweetened shredded coconut
2 teaspoons of vanilla extract
½ cup of agave syrup or honey
2 tablespoons of apple juice
1 tablespoon of ground cinnamon
1 teaspoon of ground allspice
1 pinch of freshly grated nutmeg
½ cup of chopped dried apricots

a strong cup of tea and
Miles Davis on the stereo

Musician's breakfast (homemade bread with Parma ham)

**MAKES 1
LARGE LOAF**

4 cups of whole wheat
    flour or spelt flour
1 cup of rolled oats
1 large tablespoon of
    instant yeast
1 teaspoon of sea salt
2½ cups of warm water
1 tablespoon of
    sunflower oil
1 tablespoon of honey

My beloved is a musician. This, a strong cup of tea and Miles Davis on the stereo makes him a happy fellow of a morning.

In a large mixing bowl, mix together all the dry ingredients with a wooden spoon. In a large Pyrex jug, mix together the warm water, sunflower oil and honey. Add the wet to the dry ingredients in the large bowl, mixing them together. Cover and put in a warm place. It should stay there for 20 minutes, or until it's doubled in size.

Once it has doubled, stir it with the wooden spoon until the air is gone and it is back to its original size. Trust me on this. Place the dough in an oiled 6¾-cup (9 x 5 x 2½-inch) loaf pan, and banish it back to the warm place for another 20 minutes. Preheat the oven to 375°F.

Put the bread in the oven for 45 minutes to 1 hour, depending on how it looks.

Serve with butter, mustard and a big slice of Parma ham – or, if you're like me, simply butter and marmalade.

Indian sweet potato pancakes

SERVES 2 HUNGRY PEOPLE WITH SOME LEFT OVER FOR TEA

2 egg whites
1½ cups of cooked and coarsely mashed sweet potatoes
2 scallions, chopped
1½ teaspoons of curry powder
1 pinch of ground cumin
Salt and pepper
Peanut oil

I once spent a few months in Bombay making a film that cemented two things: one, an actress I am not, but two, should all else fail I can now dance while lip-synching in Hindi. I love, love, love Indian food and, most of all, Indian breakfasts with a stress on the savory. These aren't really pancakes, more like latkes without the oil.

Beat the egg whites with a fork in a bowl. Combine everything else except the peanut oil in a big mixing bowl with your fingers, putting in the egg whites last.

Heat a frying pan or griddle, rubbed with a little bit of peanut oil, and place dollops of the mixture onto it. Remember: the bigger the pancake the longer it will take to cook, so keep them little and neat. Squash them a bit with a spatula once in the pan. They'll take about 5 minutes on each side on a medium heat, with another couple of minutes' blast on the first side at the end.

Baked haddock ramekin

Don't make this in the first throes of love or when you have people coming over. Haddock is not, and never will be, a sensory aphrodisiac. It is, however, delicious.

Preheat the oven to 350°F.

Butter two 8oz ramekins. Halve the haddock and put a piece in each ramekin. Pour the milk over the top and add a bay leaf and black pepper to each. Bake for 10 minutes. Remove from the oven and top with Cheddar. Turn on the broiler and adjust the rack. Blast the ramekins under the broiler for a few minutes. Chop some fresh parsley and sprinkle on top.

**SERVES 2 –
ALREADY IN LOVE**
Butter for greasing
1 generous piece of undyed fresh smoked haddock (11–13oz)
1 cup of milk
2 bay leaves
Freshly ground black pepper
½ cup of grated sharp Cheddar
Fresh parsley, to garnish

autumn
lunches

Spinach and watercress salad with goat's cheese

SERVES 2

2 eggs
3 cups of spinach
1 small bunch of
  watercress
½ cup of soft goat's
  cheese, crumbled
½ cup of toasted
  pumpkin seeds (or as
  many, or few, as you
  prefer)

For the dressing
1½ teaspoons of
  harissa paste
2 tablespoons of
  smoky olive oil

This is an easy salad, so I suggest buying harissa for the dressing! You can find really good harissa in any good deli or Middle Eastern shop, and all you have to do is mix it with some smoky olive oil, pour it on your salad and luxuriate in being a bit damn lazy.

Hard-boil the eggs for about 5 minutes. Wash the spinach and watercress leaves and put in a salad bowl. Peel the hard-boiled eggs, add them to your leaves and mix in the goat's cheese. Mix the harissa with the olive oil to form a dressing. Scatter the pumpkin seeds on top of the leaves and dress.

Easy peasy!

French onion soup

Purists will argue this is nothing like the real thing, which should be made with beef stock and have a great molten island of bread and cheese on top. I use vegetable stock and lose the bread – it's not as heavy, yet still as decadent and comforting. The trick is slooooooooow cooking the onions, so they impart their rich caramelly flavor to the soup. A drizzle of good balsamic vinegar also gives it a rich enigmatic taste, perfect for a blowsy autumn day.

Roughly chop the onions. In a large pot (I use a heavy-bottomed Le Creuset), melt the butter with a few glugs of olive oil on a low heat. You don't want it to burn. Make sure the bottom of the pan is covered, by swishing it around.

Pour in the onions, mix them into the oil with a wooden spoon and sweat gently for about 40 minutes. If your heat is kept to the lowest setting they won't need more oil. Sometimes this is helped by using a heat diffuser. Towards the end of the cooking, turn up the heat a bit; you want the onions to brown and caramelize, not to be charred to a crisp.

When the onions look golden and browned round the edges, pour in the stock. Turn down the heat to low again, stir, and add the balsamic vinegar. I don't know why, but this gives the soup a mellow, sweet earthiness. Let it simmer for another 15 minutes, taste, add salt and pepper if needed and then, using a ladle, pour into bowls.

Pour the cheese in when you are about to serve.

**SERVES 4
GENEROUSLY**

3 large yellow onions
1 tablespoon of butter
Slug of olive oil
2 quarts of stock –
   I use 1 quart of
   chicken stock,
   1 quart of vegetable.
   Beef is the
   traditional choice,
   but I think this is as
   good
1 tablespoon of good
   aged syrupy balsamic
   vinegar
Salt and pepper
1 cup of grated cheese
   – Gruyère is
   delicious, but
   Parmesan will
   do as well

decadent and comforting

Squid salad with char-grilled peppers and cilantro dressing

One of the best lunches I ever had was on a small boat in Greece, where the mother of the captain dove into the sea in an enormous swimming costume, surfacing triumphant holding a wiggling bag of squid. She fried them with lemon and olive oil. It was heaven. This is a tribute to her.

Char-grill the peppers in a grill pan with some olive oil. Once they are grilled and cooled slightly, cut them into thinner strips.

Chop the squid into rings, but leave the tentacles whole. Sauté in a hot frying pan with a little more olive oil until they are light golden: 2–3 minutes. Pour onto a plate and mix with the peppers.

Put the cilantro, basil, oil, garlic and lime juice in the blender and blend on high. If necessary, add a bit more lime juice. Pour over the squid and peppers and serve.

SERVES 4–6

1 large red bell pepper, quartered lengthwise, seeds removed
1 large yellow bell pepper, quartered lengthwise, seeds removed
Olive oil
Roughly 4 cups of cleaned baby squid

For the dressing
1 bunch of fresh cilantro, chopped
A few basil leaves
¼ cup of olive oil
½ a clove of garlic, peeled and chopped
Juice of 1 lime

Baked eggs with Swiss chard

SERVES 2
Butter for greasing
2 tablespoons of
  olive oil
1 cup of chopped red
  onions
1 cup of chopped
  Swiss chard
2 eggs
½ cup of crumbled
  goat's cheese

There is something about baked eggs that is redolent of the nursery tea. They are so easy and are a miniature cozy meal in themselves. Mix with Swiss chard – nutty, marvelous and oh so good for you.

Preheat the oven to 350°F. Set a rack in the lower third of the oven.

Butter two large ramekins (or a large dish if you want to bake the eggs together). Heat the olive oil in a pan until hot. Add the onions and caramelize for 10–15 minutes, being careful not to let them burn. Mix the onions with the Swiss chard and divide between the ramekins. Break an egg into each ramekin carefully, so it sits on top of the Swiss chard/onion mixture. Bake in the oven for 10 minutes.

Remove the ramekins from the oven and preheat the broiler. Scatter the goat's cheese on top and put under the broiler until the cheese is bubbling.

Swiss chard – nutty, marvelous and oh so good for you

Chicken and halloumi kebabs with chanterelles

SERVES 2

For the marinade
1 bunch of mixed
   fresh herbs, such as
   parsley and mint,
   chopped
1 clove of garlic, peeled
   and crushed
4–5 tablespoons of
   olive oil

2 skinless and boneless
   chicken breasts, each
   one cut into four
Olive oil
8oz halloumi cheese,
   cut into eight cubes
4 kebab skewers (either
   metal or wooden
   soaked in water)
Salt and pepper
3 cups of chanterelles

*For the dressing
(optional)*
Olive oil
Juice of 1 lemon

I am obsessed with halloumi cheese. I love its sharp, slightly rubbery soul, and I love it grilled and in salads. If you don't eat meat you could replace the chicken with vegetables – the first that springs to mind would be eggplant.

Make the marinade by chopping the herbs and garlic and putting in a mixing bowl with the olive oil. Add the cubed chicken, cover the bowl with plastic wrap and marinate in the refrigerator for 2 hours.

Preheat the broiler. In a medium frying pan, sauté the chicken pieces for 8–10 minutes over a low heat in 1 tablespoon of olive oil, then assemble the kebabs in the following order: chicken, halloumi, chicken, halloumi. Season to taste. Before you broil the kebabs, make sure the chicken is moist and, if needed, add more oil. Broil for 4 minutes under searing heat.

While the chicken is cooking, pan-fry the chanterelles in 1 tablespoon of olive oil for 3 minutes. Pour a mound of the mushrooms on a serving plate and lay the kebab sticks across them. You can make a separate dressing of olive oil and lemon juice if you want and pour that over the top.

Spinach barley soup

My nanny Maureen is a master soup-maker. It was almost worth being ill from time to time as a child, just in order to get a steaming bowl of comfort on the sofa in front of *The Wombles*. This is my homage to her.

Heat the oil in a heavy-bottomed pan, put in the onion and sage leaves and cook on a low heat for about 5 minutes. While that's cooking, heat the stock in another pan. Stir the spinach into the onion mixture and cook for another few minutes. Pour in the hot stock and cook, covered, on a low heat for 10 minutes. Add the barley and leave it cooking for another half an hour or until the barley is soft. Season to taste. When it is ready, ladle into bowls and sprinkle the Parmesan on top.

SERVES 4–6

3 tablespoons of olive oil
1 onion, chopped
2 large fresh sage leaves, chopped
6½ cups of vegetable stock
6 cups of spinach, washed and chopped
¾ cup of pearl barley
Salt and pepper
½ cup of grated Parmesan

Buckwheat risotto with wild mushrooms

SERVES 2

1 cup of buckwheat
    groats
Salt and pepper
2 cups of wild
    mushrooms
2 tablespoons of butter
2 tablespoons of
    olive oil
4 shallots, chopped
1 clove of garlic, peeled
    and crushed
2 tablespoons of white
    wine
¼ cup of mascarpone
    cheese

Purists, again, look away or balk, because this shouldn't really be called risotto. However, the grain is fed by stock, it's soupy, and if you really disagree, give it a new title.

Cook the buckwheat for 40 minutes in boiling salted water. Drain and put it aside. Wash and slice the mushrooms according to their size – the small ones you can leave whole, the bigger ones you may have to chop into chunks.

Heat 1 tablespoon of butter and 1 tablespoon of olive oil in a risotto pan or a deep frying pan. Add the shallots and garlic and cook on low for about 4 minutes. Season. Add your chopped mushrooms with about 1 tablespoon of white wine. Cover and continue to cook on a low heat for another 4 minutes. Put the mixture in a warm dish and don't throw away the lovely juice.

Using your risotto pan again, put the buckwheat in with the rest of the oil and butter, the mascarpone cheese and the mushroom juice. Add another tablespoon of wine and cook for 3 minutes or so, giving it a gentle stir through at the beginning to mix everything together. Put into shallow bowls and pour the mushroom mixture over the top.

autumn
suppers

Peasant soup

SERVES 4–6

1 onion, chopped

About 3 tablespoons
of olive oil

A few cloves of garlic,
unpeeled

1 carrot, chopped

1 celery stalk, chopped

2 cups of chopped kale

1 quart of vegetable or
chicken stock

1 cup of white wine

2 cups of cooked or
drained canned
cannellini beans

½–1 cup of grated
Parmesan

Something I make on a long dark afternoon to chase autumnal blues away. It's simple and endlessly variable. You could put whatever you have hanging around in it.

Begin, as always, with the onion, oil and garlic in a heavy-bottomed pan. Cook on low for about 5 minutes. Add the carrot, celery and kale and stir for another 3 minutes or so. Pour on the stock if it gets sticky before then, otherwise, add it at this stage along with the wine. Simmer on low for 20 minutes and then add the beans. Simmer for another 15 minutes, stirring occasionally, then add the Parmesan. Fish out the garlic at the end just before serving. You can make this as thick or thin as you want; go by instinct and taste, adding or taking away as you want.

Sunday roast chicken and trimmings

SERVES 4
1 medium-sized happy
   free-range chicken
Salt and pepper
A handful of finely
   chopped fresh
   tarragon and dill
Olive oil
1 lemon
1 bay leaf
6 cloves of garlic,
   unpeeled

*For the celeriac and
parsnip purée*
2 celeriac, peeled and
   cut into chunks
4 parsnips, peeled and
   cut in half
1 tablespoon of butter
1 tablespoon of crème
   fraîche

Roast chicken *is* Sunday, regardless of whether I eat it or not. There is something about that smell wafting through the house, babies balanced on laps and the comforting rustle of the papers, that wordlessly marks a day of rest and family.

Preheat the oven to 400°F.

Wash and pat dry the chicken. Season it. Gently, gently, ease the skin back from the flesh; use your hands, but begin with a knife if that's easier. You don't want to separate it entirely; you want to make room to house some herbs. Pack the finely chopped herbs under the skin. Rather than use butter, I usually just splash the chicken with olive oil and rub it in. I also tend to halve a lemon and stick the two halves in the cavity, along with a bay leaf and the whole garlic cloves, skin still on. Put the chicken in a roasting pan and into the oven. It's going to stay in there for around an hour and a half.

Put the celeriac and parsnips into some boiling salted water and cook for about 20 minutes, until tender. Drain, but save a little bit of the water for the purée and gravy – a mere splash. Pop the celeriac and parsnips into a blender, with the butter, the crème fraîche and a bit of salt and pepper. Taste and adjust the seasoning if you need too. Set aside.

About 10 minutes before the chicken is ready, boil the carrots, no longer than 5 minutes, as you want them slightly *al dente*. Drain and put to one side. In the still-hot pot, melt the butter and add the cumin, caraway seeds, ginger and sugar. Throw the carrots in and make sure they are thoroughly coated with the mixture.

Take the chicken out and make your gravy – I use the chicken juice, a little extra stock, maybe some white wine, cream, a bit of arrowroot and salt and pepper to taste. Eat and then have a nap.

For the carrots
2 medium-sized
   carrots, julienned
1 tablespoon of butter
1 teaspoon of ground
   cumin
1 teaspoon of caraway
   seeds
1 tablespoon of finely
   chopped fresh
   gingerroot
1 teaspoon of light
   brown sugar

For the gravy
A little chicken stock,
   hot
A splash of white wine
   (optional)
1 tablespoon of cream
1 tablespoon of
   arrowroot, blended
   with water
Salt and pepper

Paris mash

SERVES A FEW

3 cups of Puy lentils

1–2 tablespoons of olive oil

1 red onion, finely chopped

1 clove of garlic, peeled and chopped

½ cup of red wine

1 cup of spinach

1 cup of vegetable stock

1 tablespoon of crème fraîche

2 handfuls of mâche (lamb's lettuce)

A generous handful of both fresh parsley and cilantro

Salt and pepper

Paris mash was so named from when I used to visit my great friend, the brilliant artist Annie Morris, in her apartment on the Rue Guisarde in Paris when we were both about nineteen. We would go late to the local supermarket and buy a strange mixture of Puy lentils, salad, garlic, onions and herbs. I suppose it was like a student stone soup, originally made from whatever was in the fridge. The mash would be cooked willy-nilly, accompanied by a lot of red wine, and usually us gazing stupidly at an assortment of pretty French boys, but for some reason it was always utterly delicious.

Place the lentils in a pan and add just enough water to cover. Simmer over a low heat for 20 minutes, then drain. In a large pan, heat 1 tablespoon of the oil and add the onion. Cook on a low heat for about 10 minutes. Add the garlic and cook for 5 more minutes. Add the lentils with the red wine and cook for another 5 minutes. Add the spinach with about a ½ cup of vegetable stock and cook for another 5 minutes. If the liquid gets low, add some more stock or a bit more wine as the consistency should be slightly soupy.

Stir in the crème fraîche and 1 tablespoon of olive oil. Put the mâche in at the end and cook for a few minutes. Roughly chop the herbs and scatter them on top. Season to taste and serve as is.

The joy of this is its complete easiness, and that you can play around with it, tasting throughout the process. Serve with some warm sourdough bread to mop up the juices.

serves a few –
pretty French
boys not
mandatory

Sea bass in tarragon and wild mushroom sauce

SERVES 2
2 fillets of sea bass
Salt and pepper
Olive oil
1 cup of mixed wild
  mushrooms
¼ cup of fish stock
1 tablespoon of Pernod
  or Ricard
1 tablespoon of light
  cream
1 tablespoon of very
  finely chopped fresh
  tarragon

Tarragon is one of my favorite herbs. It has a clean aniselike flavor that makes it perfect for fish or chicken. I would plant it in my garden in London, but the neighbor's cat is partial to peeing on every herb I have while giving me a distinctly bolshy look through the window. The local farmer's market is a lot more appealing.

Preheat the oven to 400°F. Season the bass and brush with a little olive oil. It should go into the oven for just under 15 minutes, so as soon as it's in, begin your sauce.

Sauté the mushrooms in a little bit of olive oil in a non-stick pan for about 4 minutes. Add the fish stock and simmer on low for 3–4 minutes. Add the Pernod or Ricard and, when it has reduced a bit, add the cream and tarragon and stir.

Take the fish out of the oven and cover with the sauce. Serve with some crisp green beans.

Lily's stir-fry with tofu

This is my great friend Lil's staple. I stayed with her for a few months, and we lived off this and a large supply of Green & Black's chocolate.

In a large wok (or something you can sort of pretend is a wok), heat the sesame oil. Start with the cabbage as this takes longest to cook. Cook for 10 minutes. From then on you just layer up – onion next, then the tofu, a dash of tamari or soy sauce, a dash of mirin or apple cider vinegar, the carrot, zucchini, snow peas or bean sprouts and sesame seeds. Add things to your heart's content. Stir-frying should be hot and quick, and easy to the point of promiscuity.

At the end, chop up some cilantro and throw it on top, and eat on your lap watching *Mean Girls*.

Oh, the glamour.

SERVES 2

2 tablespoons of sesame oil

1 cup of shredded red cabbage

½ cup of roughly chopped onion

½ a block of firm tofu, cubed

2 tablespoons of tamari or soy sauce

1 teaspoon of mirin or apple cider vinegar

1 cup of coarsely grated carrot

1 cup of coarsely grated zucchini

1 cup of snow peas or bean sprouts

1 tablespoon of sesame seeds

A handful of chopped fresh cilantro

we lived off Lily's stir-fry and a large supply of Green & Black's

Eggplant Parmigiana

I first ate eggplant Parmigiana in New York when I was thirteen, the night we moved into our new house, sitting amid dusty boxes, rigid with jet lag and eating with a plastic fork out of a container from the Italian takeaway around the corner. The smoky eggplant, layered with sweet tomato sauce and pools of mozzarella, really woke me up.

Preheat the oven to 400°F. Cut the eggplant into ½-inch-thick slices lengthwise. Lay them on a flat surface and sprinkle them generously with sea salt. Leave for 20 minutes.

Meanwhile, in a big saucepan, heat some of the olive oil and gently sweat the onion and garlic. Don't let it burn; keep it on a low heat and keep stirring. Add the tomatoes and brown sugar and season. Simmer with the lid on for about 20 minutes. Feel free to add a tablespoon of thick syrupy balsamic vinegar, if you have any.

Put the eggplant slices on a cookie sheet in a single layer. Brush with olive oil and bake for 15 minutes until they start to turn gold.

Grease a largish baking dish with some olive oil. Remove the eggplant from the oven and arrange a layer of them in the prepared dish. Sprinkle with some basil, add some mozzarella slices, tomato sauce and then the Parmesan. Keep going in this order until you have used everything up, saving a little Parmesan and basil to sprinkle over the top. Bake for 20 minutes and serve with a green salad.

SERVES 4–6

3 medium-sized
  eggplants
Sea salt
½ cup of olive oil
1 large onion, sliced
2 cloves of garlic,
  peeled and finely
  chopped
3 (14½oz) cans of
  chopped tomatoes
1 tablespoon of light
  brown sugar
Salt and pepper
Aged balsamic vinegar,
  to taste (optional)
2 cups of chopped
  fresh basil
2 large balls of buffalo
  mozzarella, sliced
  (you could also use
  ricotta)
1 cup of grated
  Parmesan

Grilled salmon with baked onions

My mum is the queen of baked onions, and I grew up on them. There is something almost puddingy about a slow-cooked onion with the mellow sweetness that the oven coaxes out. I could also happily eat this cold the following day. (And have.)

To begin, peel the onions and boil them whole in a pan of water for 20 minutes. Preheat the oven to 350°F.

When the onions are tender, take them out of the water and cut them in half. Place them in a heatproof shallow dish, season them, add the cream and sprinkle the grated cheese on top. Put them in the oven for 25–30 minutes.

When the onions have been cooking for 15 minutes, wash and season the salmon. Pour a generous slick of oil on each fillet and squeeze the juice of half a lemon over each. Heat a grill pan and sear the salmon for about 5 minutes on each side.

By now the onions should be bubbling and golden brown on top. Serve on a plate with the salmon and a plain green salad with a sharp vinaigrette.

SERVES 2

4 small yellow onions
Salt and pepper
½ cup of light cream
½ cup of grated
    Parmesan or Gruyère
2 fat skinless fillets of
    wild salmon
Olive oil
1 lemon

winter

BREAKFASTS
Pear and ginger muffins
Scrambled tofu with cumin and shiitake mushrooms
Kedgeree with brown rice
Scrambled eggs with red chiles and vine tomatoes
Winter fruit compote
Oatmeal with apricots, manuka honey and crème fraîche
Hangover eggs
Grilled bananas with Greek yogurt and agave

LUNCHES
Warm winter vegetable salad
Chicken soup with chickpeas
Spelt pancakes filled with cream cheese and butternut squash
Pasta puttanesca
Hollers' curried parsnip soup
Char-grilled artichoke hearts with Parmesan and
    winter greens
Chestnut and mushroom soup

SUPPERS
Brown rice risotto with pumpkin, mascarpone, sage
    and almonds
My dad's chicken curry
Monkfish with saffron sauce
Fish pie with celeriac mash
Cauliflower cheese
Buttermilk chicken with smashed sweet potatoes
Christmas done as healthily as it can be

The first recollection I have of cooking, or helping the cook, was when I was about three and a half. We lived in Wandsworth, next door to a dear couple called Joyce and George. Joyce and George fostered children, so I loved going round there because there was always stuff to do or someone to play with.

My hanging out there became such a part of everyday life that George built a little mini wooden gate for me in the garden wall, so I could come and go as I pleased between the houses. The problem was, I took this invitation far too literally. Family folklore has it that my aunt Lucy had come round to babysit and was running me a bath. I apparently decided that it wasn't bath time for me, but social hour. The moment Lucy's back was turned I ran into the garden, and minutes later ambled into Joyce and George's busy kitchen stark naked.

"Evenin'. What's for dinner?" I am told I said. Lucy, meanwhile, was going out of her mind, thinking I had been kidnapped. Joyce put two and two together, rang her, and she ran over to be greeted by the sight of me, naked, stuffing my face with chips. I wouldn't leave. What I do remember is the bribe I was offered to get me back to my house. I could help Joyce stir her cake batter, and if I was good and left without a fuss, wearing the T-shirt Joyce was trying to get onto my wriggling form, then I would be allowed to come and get a piece of cake first thing in the morning.

I loved the feeling of working the big wooden spoon through the cake batter, of pouring it, thick and glossy, into the pan. I was scared but fascinated by the blast of heat from the oven, and hid behind Joyce's legs when she put the cake in to bake. I thought about the cake both during my reluctant bath and while Lucy was putting me to bed.

In the morning, there it was sitting on the kitchen table, a Victoria sponge with strawberry jam in the middle and confectioners' sugar on top. It seemed like magic, how it came together like that, light like fairies' fingers, under the oven's glare. It still does.

This naked thing turned out to be an accidental theme on and off during the first twenty-two years of my life. It became common practice when I was first modelling at nineteen or so; a hazardous by-product of my curves, as none of the sample sizes ever fitted me.

"I know!" The photographer would cry. "Let's shoot her . . . naked!"

"Here we go again," I'd think. Rather than losing weight, as you might expect from all the media focus that had begun to surround my anomalous curviness, I was instead getting rounder and rounder.

So, naked and green as the grass, I was also not cooking, as I had throughout my childhood and adolescence. Instead, I would eat lunch and dinner at restaurants, revelling in the grown-up sophistication of it all, ordering appetizers, main courses and desserts. I remember a sage friend whom I'd grown up with saying to me, "It can't be good for you eating out all the time – because restaurants want you to come back, they're going to make you the most delicious food in the world, but loaded with butter, with cream, with salt and sugar. They don't care if you get fat."

"Oh no," I'd respond, eyes round with greed. "Of course they don't use any more of those things than you and I do. They use proper ingredients, so it's not fattening at all." With that I'd plow into another round of truffled mashed potatoes laden with butter.

It was the same on airplanes. The stewardess would come round with a clinking trolley of ice cream.

"Would you like one?" she'd ask with twinkling eyes.

"Oh, yes, please," I'd say.

"That's right, you should. Gives us all hope."

It didn't matter that I wasn't hungry or didn't have a particular hankering for ice cream. I just thought I could, so I should. I was the big model. I was meant to eat, a lot. It gave other people hope and cheered them as they enjoyed their chocolate. It was a clumsy way of thinking.

Gee-Gee told me I had perfect hands for baking, because they were always cold

The more I ate, the hungrier I seemed to be. I also felt heavy, down to my bones. I didn't know how to address it, because I felt that if I became thinner it would mean I was a hypocrite, because I had talked so happily on the record about my shape, and by getting thinner, wouldn't all of that be negated? Would it mean I was a liar? It was confusing. I carried on eating; indeed, when I ordered two green curries, rice, stir-fried vegetables and soup from the local Thai restaurant I pretended that I had someone over for dinner.

"Do you want sticky rice, Bob?" I asked my phantom guest loudly, as if the nice Thai lady on the other end of the phone really cared that I was a glutton. I really knew nothing about nutrition or what was good or not so good for me. I guessed a lot, and my guessing was pretty off the mark.

Had my grandmother Gee-Gee been around (to my total heartache, she died when I was nineteen), she would have been baffled. It was Gee-Gee who first taught me to cook, in her whispering house on the Sussex coast. We began with cakes and made jam in the autumn. She told me I had perfect hands for baking, because they were (and remain) always cold. Alas, I cannot bake like she could; she was seamless. Gee-Gee was very black and white about food. You ate three meals a day, possibly a little sweet something for tea and you did "keep fit" (that's what she called it) three times a week. She was organic and sustainable before it was fashionable. Vegetables came from her garden, fish from the local fishermen on the beach and she could make appealing leftovers out of nothing, or so it seemed. Her mentality towards food was sensible and balanced. If you ate too much, which she rarely did, you walked it off on the beach for a brisk hour. "Dear heart, you can't still be hungry?" she'd ask as I wandered in and out of the kitchen after dinner, aged seventeen, looking for something, anything, to vanquish the bottomless pit of teenage hunger.

"I'm *starving*."

"Darling, you're not starving. People in Africa are starving. You've just had dinner. You're peckish."

"No. I'm *starving*." She would raise her eyes heavenward, but because she had the patience of a saint, she would say nothing. Instead she'd try and find healthy snacks.

"What about a lovely prune?"

"Yeah, no thanks."

"Some delicious All-Bran? Fiber's very good for you, you know."

"Gee-Gee, I'm not constipated! I'm hungry."

"What about a nice little toffee?"

"Oh, all right then, yes, please."

"Now shall we watch that *Thelma and Louise* film with the naughty man with the messy hair?" (Brad Pitt.)

While Gee-Gee taught me to bake, I learned the rudiments of cooking from my mum. From a young age my siblings and I always helped with Sunday lunch, the preparing of which was a sort of unspoken thing that we picked up as we went along. My mum is an instinctive cook; she rarely cooks from recipes. I do the same thing, which becomes problematic in translating a recipe for someone else. "Well, I used a pinch of this . . ."

These Sunday lunches were illustrative of that – things would be added on a whim, and sometimes Yorkshire pudding was served alongside chicken just for the hell of it. My mum made insanely good puddings with rather frilly sauces. She also imparted to me, with an old-fashioned gravity, the importance of feeding your man. "Cooking for one's man" was accompanied by a soundtrack of Dolly Parton, Crystal Gayle and possibly Stevie Wonder. It involved occasional running to the mirror between stirring things to put on lip gloss. Said man was meant to be very grateful for the bounty that was set before him, and if he wasn't, then woe betide him.

When I was about seventeen I invited a boy I adored for dinner. I asked him, if he could have anything in the world for dinner, what would it be? "Spaghetti carbonara," was the response. He came over, wolfed the spaghetti carbonara and swiftly departed, leaving me with the washing up, unkissed and a bit heartbroken.

My mum found me having a good old sob in my bedroom. "He loves my spaghetti, but he doesn't love me!" I wailed.

"Well, he's a fool then," she said, with the eternal bias of mothers.

Around the same time, I became obsessed with making the perfect baked potato (inspired, perhaps, by the golden offerings of the pub in Golders Green). I would make my friends come over after school and taste the fruits of my labor. After the first baking, I would brush the potato with olive oil and sea salt, bake it again until the skin was crisp and polished and then ready it for the next stage, which was scooping out the inside and mashing it to smoothness with a bit of butter, salt, a dash of milk and perhaps a little freshly grated nutmeg. The filling changed depending on the day. One day it would be a cheese and leek sauce with the kick of a bit of mustard; on another, a dollop of sour cream with some watercress and chives would do the trick.

Again, if Gee-Gee had been around, I think my round moment would have been much more fleeting. My parents saw it to be a phase, one that they too had been through, just not on a catwalk.

I fell into a massive bowl of pasta like a drowning man

Due to the combination of nudity, stewardesses and random public comment, I decided it was high time for a reflective sabbatical. I was twenty. I went to stay with my lovely aunt Lucy (she of the babysitting) in Los Angeles, who was and remains a great exerciser in phenomenal shape. She offered to book me a series of sessions with a trainer at a nearby gym.

"I think that might be a very good idea," I said.

"Hurrah! How exciting!" she answered. "We can go to Niketown and get running shoes."

I privately thought that Blahnik might be a bit more exciting, but kept that to myself, as I was getting so heavy that all my spindly heels kept breaking in two. "So you're a model?" the sweet, svelte redheaded trainer asked dubiously. "Well, yes," I said, trying not to hyperventilate and pass out after minute three of the treadmill.

"A plus-size model?" she asked.

"Not really. I wasn't meant to be, you see . . . oh, it doesn't matter. Yes, I suppose so."

When I got home, Lucy made me a massive bowl of pasta with pesto. I fell into it like a drowning man.

The brilliant thing about Los Angeles was that the moment people realized I wasn't an actress they lost interest in what it was that I actually did for a living. Thus I went quietly about my business, writing bad poetry, reading lots of books and going to the redhead.

Los Angeles is an unforgiving body capital if you are in the movie industry. That is clear from both the size-2 jeans that stretch across shop floors and the amount of steamed egg whites that feature heavily on breakfast menus there. But because I wasn't an actress, and didn't have any interest in steamed egg whites or size-2 jeans, the body obsession sort of passed me by. In England, where I had grown up and gained body notoriety, my sudden appetite for the gym would have been an issue. In L.A. no one was interested in me and my curvy peccadilloes. I was just another blond girl with big boobs, and therefore probably a Playmate wannabe. This disinterest was liberating. Because I wasn't thinking or talking about it all the time, my weight ceased plaguing me to quite the same degree.

The irony was that the pounds gently began to fall off, and by the time I left, three months later, I was at about the same place, bodywise, that I had started from a few years before. I felt for the first time since my career began that my body wasn't an entity separate from me. Suddenly it was within my jurisdiction again. In that time came realization number one – which was that my body belonged to me and I alone held its fate, good or bad, in my hands.

I flew back to a frosty London, buoyant, and said no to the ice cream on the plane.

Having reintroduced myself to exercise, I found another trainer in London. The reason, truthfully, why I have always had trainers is because I absolutely loathe going to the gym. I love the way it makes me feel afterwards, and I love the effect, but during the actual process itself, I am totally miserable and complain like Eeyore.

The new trainer was not like the redhead. He was militant and kind of mean. He was enormous and impenetrable like a rusting gate. He shrieked at me army-style, *"Do you want to be fit or fat?"*

"What?" I wondered why I was paying for this, and whether I was secretly a masochist.

"I said, 'Do you want to be fit or fat?'"

"Fit." I stared up at his oddly hairless nostrils.

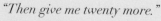

"Then give me twenty more."

Afterwards I would feel nauseous and grateful. It was all going swimmingly. I told him shyly that I didn't need to be like a twig, but that I wanted to be toned and healthy. I felt embarrassed about going to the gym; I didn't really want anyone to know, so it was all a bit surreptitious, as if I were having an affair. He was sweet in his bossy, no-nonsense way, and I came to look forward to the sessions. I trusted him, and felt like he understood why my body image had got a bit skewed.

One day he left a message on my mobile phone about an appointment the following morning. But then he forgot to hang up. These were the days where you actually had to wait for a message to finish in order to erase it. He was in the car with a friend. I heard general rustling and then his big booming voice.

"So you know who that was, right? She says that one day she wants to have a body like Cindy Crawford. Have you seen her, poor cow? If we were ever to make a workout video it would be called 'Loud and Lumpy . . .'" Here he delivered a cackle. "And in case you didn't get it, I wouldn't be Lumpy. Biggest arse I've ever seen. Big everywhere, actually."

I felt disappointed. Obviously I knew I had a big arse, otherwise I wouldn't be paying him to make it smaller. Surely there was an ethical code for trainers, a sort of Lycra Hippocratic Oath that didn't permit them to mock corpulent clients to friends? I rang him back.

"An unfortunate thing has happened, and I cannot come and see you tomorrow," I stuttered.

"You'd better have a bloody good excuse," he said.

"I do. Sadly, when you left your message, you didn't hang up the phone properly. I feel it is totally wrong of you to mock my arse, *which* I'm trying to make smaller, in the car with your friends. I understand that people have conversations that are not meant to be heard by others, but I heard that one and it made me feel weird. So I can't come and see you ever again, I'm sorry."

There was a long dramatic pause.

"Well, you are fat," he said sulkily. "So I was merely stating a fact."

"Please don't make it worse. I think we should just concede that it was a sad thing that happened and leave it at that."

"But your arse is big." He growled.

"OK. I'm going to go now."

The next day he sent me, of all things, a cardigan (size: small), with a little note. "I hope this is not too big," it said.

I developed an exercise malaise after this. What was the point? I thought. It was embarrassing and stupid. It was painful. I was having a hard time figuring out what I wanted to do long term, and how I was going to do it. Maybe I should just embrace kaftans and be the local round eccentric?

I began cooking again, as I had a lot of time on my hands. I lived in a funny little cottage with an ancient gas oven that was one of the best ovens I've ever had. I had dinner parties and cooked standard nursery staples for days in advance, closeted away in my lichen-colored kitchen, making heaving pots of things. I ate a lot and grazed all day on the things I cooked, and had a few nice but unsuitable boyfriends over this period whom I fed like Christmas geese.

Someone offered me a part in a film, and then another. I wasn't very good. I thought with classes I could maybe get better. I auditioned for a big ensemble Shakespearean thing, and wonder of wonders, got called back to screen test. I waited with my breath held for a week. The director wrote me a sweet letter. The studio had passed on me.

I was twenty-one; I had no money and was thinking about waitressing again and applying to college. The phone rang and it was my agent, telling me of a well-paid week-long job in a faraway country. I thanked my lucky stars. "There will be a press day, and they will ask you about your body," she said.

They did ask me about my body. Incessantly. But I didn't care, because as soon as I was back, I took my faraway-country money and checked in to the wonderful Ballymaloe House in Ireland, which I had read about in every cooking magazine, but never been to. Ballymaloe is run by the fearless cook Darina Allen. It is a Georgian house a few miles from the sea and the food is out of this world. It was interesting because although I was there for under a week, and was eating substantially at every meal, I left thinner than when I arrived. This was because I was eating simply and

I began cooking again, making heaving pots of things

well: Gee-Gee style, three meals, freshly prepared with no sinister chemical ingredients, no picking, and every afternoon I'd go for a long walk by the sea. I had breakfasts of sunflower-colored scrambled eggs with a slice of fresh whole wheat soda bread with butter. Lunch was a delicious soup and a large salad, with perhaps a thin sliver of a tarte tatin, and for supper I would have fresh fish with an abundance of vegetables.

Back home I carried on eating like this, cooking every night, and not just eating because I was bored. Whereas my cooking before had been safe and starchy, this new lease was healthy, bold and adventurous. I became more confident with each thing I cooked. I had always loved supermarkets, and now I went to them armed with my imagination and an eye for color. I picked up the things that I was previously afraid of cooking – spiny artichokes, garnet-colored beets, skate wings.

I chose what I was going to cook in the morning and I went for it. If it was raining outside, I cooked stews and bouillabaisses; if the sun shone, if it snowed, I cooked. I discovered the joy of cooking, and the joy inherent in cooking for people I loved. It is one of the purest pleasures around, and like reading and bicycle riding, it is one of those things that once you know how to do, you don't forget. It is something that stays with you for the rest of your life. What I came away with after that up-down maelstrom time in England impacted how I lived life after it.

I learned the foundations of good eating, and began to find the balance of it. I realized there wasn't some secret code to crack, that the "secret" could be found in the straightforward mentality of my grandmother, and most grandmothers the world over. Responding to fad trends in eating (or being a trend because of your eating!) can be potentially problematic and confusing. Trends taper off quickly; they change like the wind. There are trends all over the place in art and music, fashion and film and, certainly in the past twenty years, massive trends in diet. Who would have thought fifty years ago that an entire food group would be maligned and vilified, and for a spell removed from the everyday diets of millions of people? I write of the carbohydrate, that poor misunderstood thing. Cabbage soup, anyone? Or a diet consisting of grape-

I learned the foundations of good eating and realized there wasn't some secret code to crack

fruit and hard-boiled eggs? Chemicals instead of fat? Our ancestors would have been rolling in the aisles. The tried-and-tested old formulas (about food, or anything else for that matter) tend to be the most faithful; they are the ones to which we return.

In order to come at something from a strong and certain place, we have to have a good sound foundation. Sometimes, because of circumstances, that's not something we're armed with, and if we're not, we have to learn it pretty quickly. Learning it can be messy and painful, humorous and rewarding. The learning is part of the experience. It's what makes us who we are; human, flawed and, oh God, ready to learn some more. . . .

winter
breakfasts

Pear and ginger muffins

Really rather virtuous, and ideal if you are hankering for something sweet, but have been overdoing it a bit; these are airy-fairy spongy little things without the density of a traditional muffin. You might want to serve them alongside something heartier, or should you want a wisp of a breakfast, they'll do on their own.

Preheat the oven to 375°F. Grease a 12-hole muffin pan (preferably nonstick) with sunflower oil. (You can also use individual paper liners which can look very pretty to serve them in – and, as an optional extra, add a slice of pear to the top of the muffin mix as a lovely garnish.)

Sift the baking powder, baking soda, ginger, cinnamon and nutmeg into a large mixing bowl. Stir in the spelt flour and the oats. Make a well in the middle of the dry ingredients and add in all the wet ingredients, the diced pear and the raisins. Stir very gently, until all the dry ingredients are folded into the batter. Pour the batter into the pan, filling each cup two-thirds full.

Put in the oven and bake for 25–30 minutes, until the tops of the muffins are brown. Serve warm with apple butter if you can get it; it's also delicious with marmalade.

MAKES 12 MUFFINS

Sunflower oil
2 teaspoons of baking powder
1 teaspoon of baking soda
1 teaspoon of ground ginger
1 teaspoon of ground cinnamon
¼ teaspoon of freshly grated nutmeg
1¼ cups of spelt flour
1½ cups of rolled oats
1 cup of pear fruit purée (I use organic baby food!)
4 egg whites, lightly beaten
½ cup of plain yogurt
¾ cup of agave syrup or honey
1 firm pear, peeled, cored and diced
¾ cup of raisins

Scrambled tofu with cumin and shiitake mushrooms

SERVES 2

1 tablespoon of sesame oil

1 cup of chopped shiitake mushrooms

Salt and pepper

½ a block of firm tofu

1 heaping teaspoon of ground cumin

1 tablespoon of chopped fresh thyme, plus extra to serve (optional)

I didn't really understand tofu until I moved to America. It is a bland protein sponge, but it makes a perfect canvas for anything you want to flavor it with. It comes in different textures and you can do anything with it – scramble it, bake it or grill it. Useful to have around for any noncarnivores.

Heat the oil in a pan and pan-sear the mushrooms. Season and set aside. Add a little more oil to the pan and crumble the tofu in with your fingers and cook until it looks like scrambled eggs. Stir in the cumin and thyme with a wooden spoon. Make sure the tofu is coated evenly.

Spoon it onto two plates and pour the mushrooms on top, adding some more thyme if it pleases you.

Kedgeree with brown rice

The Victorians would have a fit, but I find brown rice a lighter, nuttier alternative to white for this filling breakfast/brunch.

Poach the haddock in a little milk with a bay leaf for about 5 minutes, then skin and flake it.

In a large pan, heat some olive oil and sweat the onion, leek and curry powder for about 5 minutes. Add the cooked rice and mix well, with some more olive oil and a bit of stock to keep it moist. Add the flaked haddock bits.

If you are going to serve in your big pan, which I, not very posh, would, add the eggs and the cream, and give it a final throw with a big wooden spoon so everything is covered. Taste and season, adding a whisper of paprika. Cover it in fresh parsley.

If you are transferring to a grand bowl, add the eggs at the end in a tidy fashion, and throw the parsley on with more restraint!

SERVES 4

1 large (about 1lb) haddock fillet
A little milk
A bay leaf
Olive oil
1 small onion, chopped
1 small leek, chopped
1 tablespoon of curry powder
3 cups of cooked brown rice (about 1 cup uncooked)
Vegetable or fish stock
4 hard-boiled eggs, quartered
2 tablespoons of light cream
Salt and pepper
Dash of paprika
A great big handful of fresh parsley, chopped

Scrambled eggs with red chiles and vine tomatoes

SERVES 2

4–6 small tomatoes on the vine

Salt and pepper

Olive oil

1 tablespoon of butter

1 red chile, deseeded and finely chopped

4 eggs

One of my oldest and best friends is Emma, 5 feet to my 5 feet 10. She is the only person I know who actually owns about thirty rain hats (she has a morbid fear of getting wet) and she has the feet of a tiny fairy. When my equally dainty-of-foot grandmother Gee-Gee died, Emma inherited all her shoes and gloves, wearing them with the same panache as their former owner. She is a magpie for any jewel and these eggs with a kick are her suggestion.

Preheat the oven to 375°F.

Put the tomatoes on a small roasting pan, season and splash with olive oil. Put them in the oven for 15 minutes.

In a saucepan, heat the butter on low and cook the chopped chile for 2–3 minutes. Whisk the eggs and season, then pour into the saucepan, stirring continuously. When they are softly scrambled, remove from the heat. Take out the tomatoes and break the vine in half, one for each plate of scrambled eggs.

Winter fruit compote

You will need to start this the night before, as soaking can redeem even the most pitiful dried fruit into plump juicy heaven.

In a mixing bowl, combine the fruit and add to it 2 cups of cooled Lapsang tea and the orange juice. Give it a stir, cover, and leave overnight in the fridge. In the morning – miraculously fat, soused fruit.

Pour the fruit mix into a saucepan with the cinnamon stick, using a little more orange juice if it has greedily drunk all the liquid, and cook on a low heat for a few minutes. Put yogurt in a bowl and pour the fruit mixture on top, sprinkling the almonds on top of that.

NOTE:
If you are serving only one or two, I suggest keeping it covered in the fridge and warming up a little each morning.

SERVES 6–8
1 cup of dried pitted
  prunes
1 cup of dried apricots
1 cup of golden raisins
A pot of Lapsang
  Souchong tea
½ cup of orange juice,
  plus a little extra
1 cinnamon stick
Yogurt, to serve
½ cup of sliced
  almonds, toasted

Oatmeal with apricots, manuka honey and crème fraîche

SERVES 2

A handful of dried
   apricots
1 cup of orange juice
1 cinnamon stick
1 cup of rolled oats
2 cups of water or milk
1–2 tablespoons of
   manuka or other
   honey
1–2 tablespoons of
   crème fraîche

I am happy to eat oatmeal for lunch, supper or breakfast, and sometimes do if I've been on a trip and there's nothing in the fridge. Manuka honey is wickedly expensive but apparently packed full of antibacterial agents, and I'm a sucker for anything delicious that's meant to be good for you in the process. Cynics may sniff, and they can substitute another honey.

First, poach the apricots in the orange juice with a cinnamon stick. This should take about 5 minutes.

In a separate saucepan, cook the oats – two cups of water (or milk, if you prefer) to one cup of oats. If you are using classic rolled oats, it should take about 5 minutes. Pour the orange juice away and put the apricots in the oatmeal. Serve in two bowls with a spoonful of honey and a spoonful of crème fraîche in each.

Hangover eggs

For when nothing but a fry-up will do. It's not pretty, but it does the trick. You can add whatever you feel like to it – I find the saltier and spicier the better, under the circumstances. A can of Coke completes the bacchanalia, as does some bad television and a lie-down.

Pour a little oil into a frying pan over a low heat. Crack the eggs into the pan. Add the cheese. Wilt the spinach with the mixture and add a liberal dose of Tabasco if, like me, you love it. Mash it all up, take off the heat and mix it with the chopped avocado. Make it into a sandwich. Rest.

SERVES 1
A splash of olive oil
2 eggs
A few crumbled pieces of cheese (something sharp, like Cheddar)
A handful of spinach
A few drops of Tabasco sauce
½ an avocado, chopped
2 slices of a bready thing – a roll split in half, for example

Grilled bananas with Greek yogurt and agave

SERVES 2

2 ripe bananas
1 tablespoon of agave
  syrup or honey
Rum (optional)
1 cup of plain low-fat
  Greek yogurt

My grandfather used to make a snack for us when we were little that was simply a mashed banana with a spoonful of olive oil. It's an acquired taste, but one I still love. This is equally good and probably less apt to bring on a chorus of "Urgh! What's *that?*"

Preheat the broiler. Peel the bananas and slice lengthwise. Put the four halves in a foil-lined broiler pan and drizzle the agave syrup or honey on top. If it's a rowdy sort of breakfast, you could also add some rum. Place under the hot broiler for a few minutes, until the bananas are brown and sizzling. Then put in two bowls with some yogurt and mash it all up.

winter
lunches

Warm winter vegetable salad

SERVES 2

1 red onion
1 sweet potato
2 carrots
2 parsnips
1 celeriac
2 beets
Salt and pepper
Olive oil
A handful of chopped
  walnuts
A handful of crumbled
  feta cheese

For the dressing
2 tablespoons of olive
  oil
1 handful of fresh
  parsley, chopped
1 tablespoon of
  balsamic vinegar
1 teaspoon of
  Dijon mustard
A squeeze of lemon
  juice (optional)

When the ground is covered by frost, and the days are half eaten by darkness, this salad of rich colors and earthy tastes brings to the table a vibrant reminder of what lies beneath us.

Preheat the oven to 425°F. Peel and chop the vegetables into wedges. Put them in a roasting pan, season them, then give them a healthy shower of olive oil. Cook them for about 30 minutes, turning them a couple of times. Five minutes before they are ready, put the walnuts on a cookie sheet, pop in the oven and toast them.

Pour the vegetables into a dish and sprinkle the feta on top. Make a dressing with the olive oil, parsley, balsamic vinegar, mustard and a squeeze of lemon juice, if you like. Dress the vegetables and sprinkle the warm toasted walnuts on top.

Chicken soup with chickpeas

SERVES 6

1 medium onion,
  chopped
2 tablespoons of olive
  oil
½ teaspoon of ground
  cinnamon
½ teaspoon of ground
  ginger
¾ teaspoon of ground
  turmeric
1 pinch of ground
  cumin
1 rutabaga or turnip,
  peeled and chopped
2 celery stalks,
  chopped
2 quarts of chicken
  stock
1½lb skinless and
  boneless chicken
  thighs, chopped
15oz can of chickpeas,
  drained and rinsed
Salt and pepper
Chopped fresh parsley
  or cilantro, to serve

I love making soups, both the ritual of it and the cozy feel of something brewing and simmering as you go about your morning. This is warmth and comfort in a bowl.

In a big deep soup pan, sweat the onion in some olive oil on a low heat. Add all of the spices and stir for a few minutes. Throw in the rutabaga or turnip and the celery and let it cook for about 10 minutes, until the vegetables are tender. Add the stock and the chicken and cook for 15 more minutes. Add the chickpeas and cook for another 10 minutes, always at a low simmer. Season. Serve with parsley or cilantro and a splash of earthy olive oil.

Spelt pancakes filled with cream cheese and butternut squash

There is something childishly wonderful about pancakes. They are easy to make but tangibly satisfying in their golden rounds on a plate. These are good if you have a non–meat eater in your midst. You can substitute goat's cheese and herbs or whatever you have around for the filling.

First, make the filling. Mix the cooked butternut squash in with the cream cheese and add the orange zest and parsley. Set aside.

Make the pancakes by mixing the flour, egg, milk and 1 tablespoon of olive oil together until you have a smooth batter. Heat 1 tablespoon of olive oil in a frying pan and add a ladleful of batter. You want the pancakes to be thick enough to hold the filling but not so fat that they are lumpy – a sort of plumped-up crêpe. When they are brown and lacy on each side, remove from the heat and put them on a plate, adding the filling.

NOTE:
You can eat them as is, or you could make a cheesy béchamel sauce and bake them at 350°F for 10 minutes with the sauce on top.

SERVES 2

For the filling
½ cup of cooked, drained and diced butternut squash
½ cup of soft cream cheese
1 teaspoon of orange zest
1 teaspoon of chopped fresh parsley

For the pancakes
1 cup of spelt flour
1 egg
½ cup of milk
2 tablespoons of olive oil

Pasta puttanesca

SERVES 2

For the sauce
3 tablespoons of
  olive oil
1 clove of garlic, peeled
  and chopped
½ a fresh red chile,
  deseeded and
  chopped
14½oz can of chopped
  tomatoes, drained
4 anchovy fillets
½ teaspoon of light
  brown sugar
  (optional)
½ cup of black olives,
  pitted
2 large tablespoons of
  chopped fresh
  parsley

2 cups of spelt penne

Whore's pasta – was ever a name so good? It's perfect for it: edgy, spicy and just the right side of wrong, conjuring up Neapolitan streets and dangerous women in tight dresses.

First, make the musky, heady sauce. In a pan, heat 2 tablespoons of the olive oil and sweat the garlic and the chile. You really don't want the garlic to burn, otherwise it will become bitter. Add the tomatoes and simmer on low. In a pestle and mortar, grind the anchovies with the remaining olive oil into a paste. Add to the sauce and carry on simmering for about 20 minutes. You could add half a teaspoon of brown sugar here; taste and decide.

Cook the pasta as directed on the box, until it is *al dente*. Add the olives to the sauce and serve with a big handful of parsley, and pretend you're in a steamy restaurant in a winding alleyway in Naples.

Hollers' curried parsnip soup

SERVES 4

4 large parsnips
1 medium onion, chopped
1 clove of garlic, peeled and crushed
Olive oil
1 tablespoon of curry powder
2 cups of chicken stock
2 tablespoons of light cream
A handful of chopped fresh chives
Salt and pepper
A handful of chopped fresh parsley

My dad, Julian Holloway, is lovingly known as Hollers. He cooks like a dream, and whenever he cooks from a recipe he always wants it to look like the picture. In the sixties he was the manager of a cabaret supper club in London, and when the chef quit, he took over the kitchen until they found a new one. There was a mutiny from the patrons when they found out he wouldn't be cooking their steak anymore.

First, peel and chop the parsnips, cutting them into rough chunks.

In a large soup pan, gently sweat the onion and garlic in 1 tablespoon of olive oil. Add the curry powder and stir. Pour the chicken stock into the pan and add the parsnips. Bring to a boil and then simmer until the parsnips are tender, around 15–20 minutes. Purée and put back into the soup pan, adding the cream and the chives. Season and serve garnished with the chopped parsley.

Char-grilled artichoke hearts with Parmesan and winter greens

Artichokes remind me of tropical flowers, and they are spiky little miracles. The bitter winter salad greens marry well with the sweet nutty Parmesan and the soft green heart of the artichoke.

First, the artichokes – you can either buy them already char-grilled from a good supermarket or deli, or you can buy four artichokes, steam them in a pan for 20 minutes, remove the hearts and pop them under the broiler with some olive oil for 8 minutes. The choice is entirely yours.

Arrange the greens and radishes on two plates. Make the dressing by combining the lemon juice, olive oil and fresh mint. Put the artichoke hearts and Parmesan on top of the greens, dress and add the toasted pine nuts.

SERVES 2

4 large artichoke hearts, quartered
Mixed winter salad greens – chicory and radicchio work well here
½ cup of thinly sliced radishes
A good hunk of Parmesan, shaved
2 tablespoons of toasted pine nuts

For the dressing
Juice of 1 lemon
2 tablespoons of olive oil
A handful of chopped fresh mint

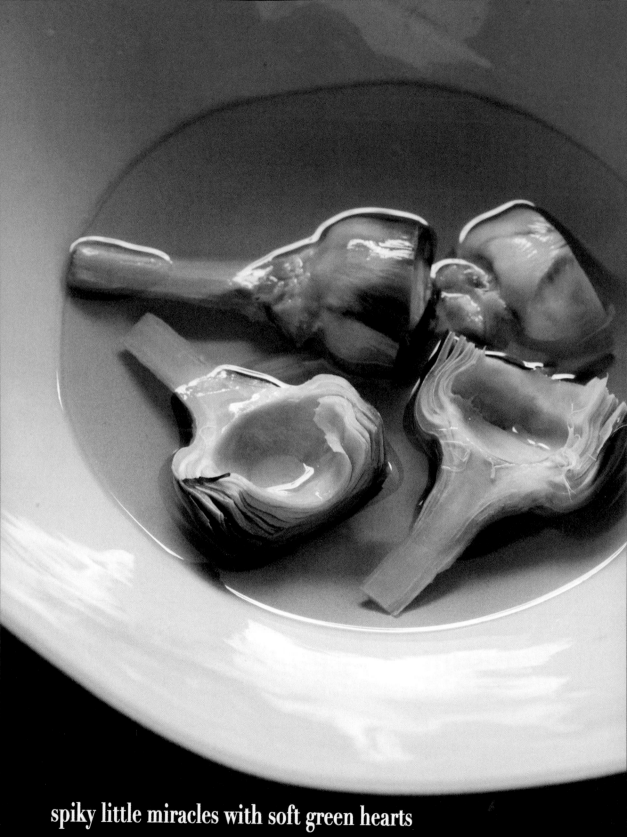

spiky little miracles with soft green hearts

Chestnut and mushroom soup

This always reminds me of Christmas menus in posh hotels. Perhaps it's the sherry, reminiscent of blue-rinsed ladies in finely upholstered armchairs.

First, sweat the onion in some olive oil; after a few minutes add the chopped mushrooms and cook on a low heat for a few minutes. Add the sherry – you should be hit by that lovely sugar waft. Season a little. Add the stock and cook on a low heat again for another 15 minutes.

Add the chestnuts and cook for another 15 minutes. Let the mixture cool a bit, then transfer to a blender and purée. Put it back in the pan – you could add a tablespoon of cream if you want. If not, toss a little chopped parsley on top, and off you go.

NOTE:
For bacon lovers, a bit of bacon or pancetta would also be pretty good, very crispy and sprinkled on top.

SERVES 4
1 small onion, chopped
Olive oil
2 cups of mixed
    mushrooms,
    chopped
1 tablespoon of sherry
Salt and pepper
1 quart of stock –
    vegetable or chicken
1 cup of canned
    chestnuts (Clement
    Faugier's are very
    good) or fresh
    chestnuts, roasted
    and peeled
1 tablespoon of cream
    (optional)
Chopped fresh parsley,
    to garnish

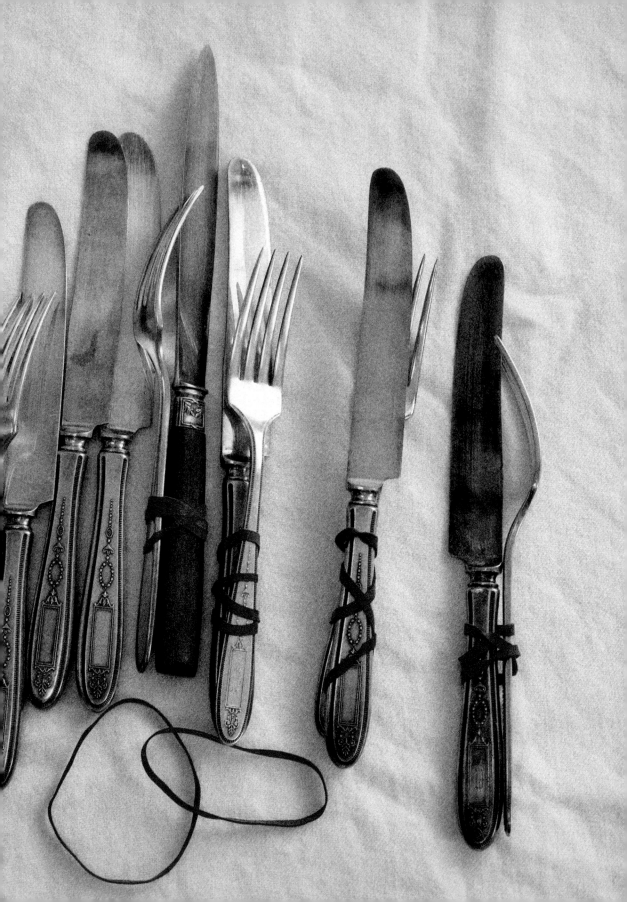

winter
suppers

Brown rice risotto with pumpkin, mascarpone, sage and almonds

Brown rice is not the same as arborio, so you won't have the same texture – this will be nuttier and less plump. However, the pumpkin and cheese are there to give it a soft cushion and it still has that touch of the nursery to it – cozy and delicious. This does take a while and some stirring, but if you have time, a friend and a glass of wine, it is effortless and quite meditative somehow.

In a risotto pan, sweat the onion and garlic for a few minutes in 1 tablespoon of olive oil. Add the rice and stir well for a few minutes, making sure it's evenly coated. Keep the heat on low. Add a cup of warmed stock. Stir until it is absorbed.

Keep doing this for about 35 minutes – the rice will just drink up the stock. Taste, and if the texture is not soft enough, keep adding the warm stock. Brown rice takes about 40 minutes to cook.

When the rice is soft and soupy, stir in the pumpkin purée. Then add the mascarpone and stir again. When it is ready, serve with the sage and toasted almonds on top.

SERVES 2

- ½ cup of finely chopped onion
- ½ a clove of garlic, peeled and finely chopped
- A few tablespoons of olive oil
- 1 cup of brown rice
- 3–4 cups of vegetable or chicken stock, warmed
- ½ cup of cooked, puréed pumpkin
- 1 tablespoon of mascarpone
- 1 tablespoon of finely chopped fresh sage
- A handful of toasted sliced almonds

My dad's chicken curry

SERVES 4

1 large onion

2 serrano chiles, deseeded (or less if you like it less hot)

2 cloves of garlic, peeled

2 tablespoons of grated fresh gingerroot

2 tablespoons of olive oil

2 teaspoons of curry powder

4 skinless and boneless chicken breasts

Salt and pepper

14oz can of light unsweetened coconut milk

1 bunch of fresh cilantro, chopped

Hollers is back! He would serve this with some basmati rice and some quickly steamed cauliflower with chopped mint, hopefully to Diane Lane, whom he's quite partial to.

Finely chop the onion, chiles and garlic, add the grated ginger and sweat in the oil for a few minutes. Add the curry powder and stir for a few minutes. Chop the chicken breasts up into bite-sized pieces and add to the mixture. Cook for another few minutes and season to taste.

Pour the coconut milk over the chicken and simmer on a low heat until the chicken is properly cooked, about 20 minutes. Scatter the chopped cilantro on top.

Serve with cauliflower that has been boiled with mint leaves, and some basmati rice.

Monkfish with saffron sauce

Clever old saffron: all it takes is a few threads to stain a sauce (and your fingers) a burnished yellow. This dish reminds me of old-fashioned French restaurants.

In a big sauté pan, heat the olive oil and add the scallions, sweating them for a minute or two. Add the fish, cooking for 3 or so minutes on each side. Pour in the wine and lemon juice and cook for another 10 minutes, covered.

Stir in the cream and saffron threads and cook for a couple of minutes, or until slightly thickened. Season everything. Transfer onto plates and serve, garnished with a bit of parsley, with some quinoa or lovely *al dente* broccoli rabe.

SERVES 2

2 tablespoons of olive oil
2 scallions, white parts only, chopped
1½lb of monkfish fillets
½ cup of white wine
1 tablespoon of lemon juice
2 tablespoons of heavy cream
5 threads of saffron
Salt and pepper
1 small bunch of parsley, chopped

Fish pie with celeriac mash

SERVES 2

For the celeriac mash
2 small celeriac
A little milk
Butter
Salt and pepper

Olive oil
½ cup of chopped
  onions
2 leeks, white parts
  only, chopped
1 cup of sliced
  mushrooms
1 cod fillet (about
  13oz), cut into
  chunks, or a mix of
  half salmon, half cod
1 cup of raw peeled
  shrimp
1½ cups of milk
1 bay leaf
1 tablespoon of butter
2 tablespoons of
  arrowroot
2 tablespoons of
  chopped fresh
  parsley
1 tablespoon of
  chopped fresh dill
1 slug of white wine
  (optional)

Give me a fish pie with peas (preferably mushy) and I'll be as happy as a clam. Yum.

First, make the celeriac mash. Peel the celeriac and cut into chunks, then boil until tender. Transfer to a blender, add a little milk, a knob of butter and some salt and pepper and whiz to a purée. Put in a bowl and set aside.

In a sauté pan, heat 1 tablespoon of olive oil and sweat the onions and leeks for a few minutes. Remove to a plate. In the same frying pan, cook the mushrooms for a few minutes until lightly golden. Put them to the side with the onions and leeks.

Place the fish and shrimp in a larger pan, cover with the milk and add the bay leaf. Poach for no longer than 4 minutes. Remove the fish from the pan and put to the side but keep the milk. Strain the milk into a Pyrex jug as you are about to use it again.

In your big pan, melt the butter on a low heat and gently stir in the arrowroot until you have a roux. Slowly pour in the reserved milk. Add the herbs, onions, leeks, mushrooms and the fish. You could also add a slug of white wine here. Make sure everything is covered.

Pour the mixture into a baking dish and cover with the mashed celeriac. If you are baking it right away, it needs only 10 minutes in a 350°F preheated oven; if you are cooking the fish pie from cold, it will take about 30 minutes.

Cauliflower cheese

SERVES 2

More rouxy – béchamel – Mornay business!

For the béchamel
2 cups of milk
1 bay leaf
1 slice of onion
A few peppercorns
2 parsley sprigs
2 tablespoons of butter,
    plus a little extra if
    needed
2–3 tablespoons of
    arrowroot, plus a
    little extra if needed

1 cauliflower
1 cup of grated cheese
    – sharp Cheddar or
    Gruyère
½ teaspoon of mustard
Salt and pepper

Preheat the oven to 350°F. First, make the bastardized béchamel. In a saucepan, bring to the boil the milk, bay leaf, onion, peppercorns and parsley. Simmer on low for 5 minutes and then remove and strain out the vegetables. Keep the milk to one side.

In the same saucepan, melt the butter on low and slowly add the arrowroot, stirring continuously. Add the milk, still stirring. When it has the right consistency (and you'll be able to tell, and can add more butter or arrowroot if necessary), take it off the heat.

Remove the green outer leaves of the cauliflower and cut the head into quarters. Put it in a saucepan with only a few inches of salted water. Cover and cook for about 15 minutes. Remove and put in a baking dish. Mix the cheese and mustard into the sauce, season, and pour on top. Bake in the oven for another 15 minutes or so, until the top is bubbling and golden.

Buttermilk chicken with smashed sweet potatoes

Buttermilk can tenderize the most stubborn of chicken breasts. I think this was probably one of the first things I ever cooked as a child – indeed, it's that simple. Sweet potatoes are packed full of vitamins and antioxidants, and children seem to find them less alarming mashed.

SERVES 2

1 cup of buttermilk
½ teaspoon of dry mustard
1 tablespoon of honey or agave syrup
2 skinless and boneless chicken breasts
2 sweet potatoes
1 tablespoon of olive oil
Salt and pepper

Make a marinade for the chicken by mixing the buttermilk, mustard and honey or agave syrup. Cover the chicken in the mixture and put it in the fridge overnight. A good way is to put everything in a large plastic bag; this way the chicken doesn't dry out and is completely coated in the marinade.

Preheat the broiler. Wash the sweet potatoes carefully and leave the skins on. Quarter them and cook in a saucepan of boiling water for 15 minutes or until tender. Remove from the water and semi-mash them with a fork and some oil and salt and pepper.

Put the chicken in a broiler pan and cook it for about 10 minutes on each side or until the juices run clear. Serve on the smashed sweet potatoes.

Christmas done as healthily

(without being drab and monochrome – what would be the point of that?)

I love Christmas. It makes me childish and silly and excited. I love midnight Mass, I love carols, I love the Queen's speech and *The Railway Children* on television. I love chocolate coins and oranges. Few things make me happier than Christmas, as long as there are no warring relations.

Boxing Day is sometimes even better than Christmas, because the pressure is off. You can wear your pajamas all day and eat leftovers, and you don't have to smile gaily if you don't want to. You still don't have to work, and you don't have as much washing up. Everyone is sleepy and replete from the day before so they can be left to their own devices or to play with their presents.

I used to be terrified of cooking turkey as there was so much fuss and secrecy surrounding it. It really isn't that difficult – don't be terrified. Get

as it can be

a guide from your butcher, but basically a small turkey needs about an hour and forty-five minutes, a medium one about three hours, and a big one about four and a half. It should be cooked at 400°F for the first 30 minutes, and at 350°F thereafter, and you should baste it a lot to keep it tender. (To begin with, season your turkey and butter it as you would a chicken.) Nigella Lawson recommends starting breast-side down, and that does really seem to help, as the fat deposits in the turkey are in the back, and cooking breast-side down first allows the fat to drip down through the bird. Turn it the right way up about 40 minutes before you take it out of the oven.

I've given you stove-top vegetables, as depending on the size of both your oven and your turkey it could complicate matters having to share oven space. The vegetables and cornbread you can also do the day before, to make life easier, and keep that sweating maniacal fever at bay.

Cornbread stuffing

SERVES 6

Sunflower oil

¾ cup of buttermilk

2 eggs

½ cup of puréed sweet
   potato

1 cup of cornmeal

1 cup of spelt flour

1 tablespoon of baking
   powder

2 tablespoons of light
   brown sugar

1 good pinch of sea salt

For the stuffing

1 egg, beaten, to bind

A good handful of
   cranberries, fresh,
   dried or frozen

2 tablespoons of
   orange juice

1 pinch of freshly
   grated nutmeg

Preheat the oven to 375°F. Grease an 8-inch square or round baking pan with a little sunflower oil. In a large bowl, mix together the buttermilk, eggs and puréed sweet potato. Sift in the dry ingredients and gently mix them together. Pour into the pan and bake for 25 minutes.

Assuming you are doing this the day before, eat some of the cornbread. Then crumble up a good 2 cups of it and mix it with the beaten egg, a handful of cranberries, the orange juice and a pinch of nutmeg. That's going to be your stuffing. Mix well and stuff in the turkey neck end (which should be washed).

Christmas red cabbage

Preheat the oven to 300°F. Prepare the cabbage: discard any tough leaves and shred – you can do this in a food processor if you like. In a big casserole (I use a big old Le Creuset), start making layers: cabbage, onion, apple, salt and pepper, interspersed with a sprinkling of the garlic, caraway seeds and brown sugar. Keep going until there are no more ingredients. Pour on top the vinegar, cider, a sniff of port and the butter. Cover and let it cook in the oven for around 3 hours.

This is easy as pie to reheat, so make it the day before as it also lets everything sit and soak.

SERVES 6

2lb of red cabbage
1lb of onions, thinly sliced
1lb of apples, peeled, cored and thickly sliced
Salt and pepper
2 cloves of garlic, peeled and finely chopped

2 tablespoons of caraway seeds
3 tablespoons of light brown sugar
3 tablespoons of white wine or apple cider vinegar
¼ cup of apple cider
A splash of port
2 tablespoons of butter

Turnip and rutabaga purée

Peel the turnip and rutabaga and chop into rough chunks. Boil for about 20 minutes. Drain and put into the food processor with a little milk, a knob of butter and some salt and pepper. Purée. Transfer to a nice baking dish and serve as is. If you're making this the night before, pop the baking dish into the oven (at 325°F) about 30 minutes before serving.

SERVES 6

1lb of turnip
1lb of rutabaga
Milk
Butter
Salt and pepper

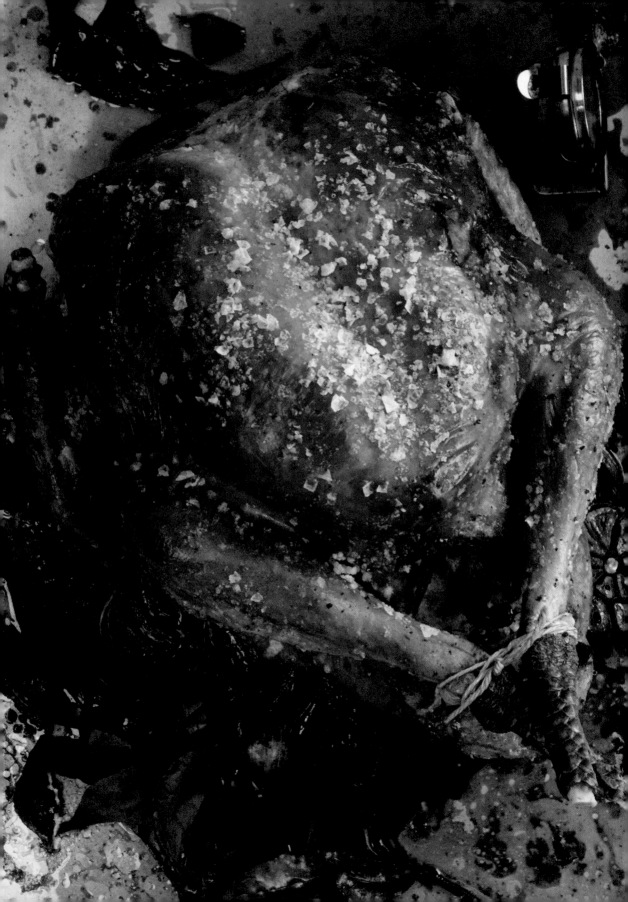

Christmas Day . . .

Assuming you're serving six, and lunch is at one, put your stuffed turkey in a roasting pan at about 10:45 a.m., having preheated the oven to 400°F. Cook at this temperature for 30 minutes, then reduce the temperature to 350°F and cook for another 2 hours. Set the table, check on the turkey occasionally and baste it as necessary. If you want some more vegetables you could do some Brussels sprouts and add some canned chestnuts and butter at the end, or you could also do green beans with some sliced almonds – whatever you think.

For dessert I would serve the chocolate chestnut soufflé cake found in the desserts section (page 268), served with some whipped cream and a healthy lace of rum. It is, after all, Christmas.

spring

BREAKFASTS
Grilled papaya with lime
Coquette's eggs
Swiss muesli
Scrambled tofu with pesto and spinach
Lemon and ricotta spelt pancakes
Grilled figs with ricotta and thyme honey
Rhubarb compote with orange-flower yogurt and pistachios

LUNCHES
My mama's baked acorn squash
Crab and fennel salad
Teddy's lettuce soup
Asparagus soup with Parmesan
Zucchini and watercress soup
Baby vegetable fricassee
Fava bean salad with pecorino and asparagus

SUPPERS
Sea bass with black olive salsa and baby zucchini
Pan-fried orange halibut with watercress purée
Hortense's fish soup
Crusted rack of lamb for Luke
Char-grilled scallops on pea purée
Turmeric tofu with cherry tomato quinoa pilaf
Chicken stew with green olives
Shrimp, avocado, grapefruit, watercress and
   pecan salad

The New York of adolescent memory still held me in its thrall. So why not rediscover it? Why not up sticks, pack a trunk and *move* there for adventure's sake? Unencumbered by responsibility, bar needing a job, twenty-one seemed the best age to just do it. Although I arrived in New York in the autumn of 1999, it was a spring of sorts; a green novice beginning.

I celebrated my twenty-second birthday there, on a rooftop in the Lower West Side, dancing to Donna Summer in a black lace ball gown that I had borrowed that day from a fashion shoot. At midnight I was Cinderella, whipping it off and swapping it for a pair of jeans in order to get it back to the kind stylist who was flying back to England at 6:00 a.m. Weaving across Fifth Avenue in a perilous pair of Louboutins, I ran into the Four Seasons Hotel, handing over the still-warm bundle of lace to a sleepy concierge.

Three of my friends had moved to New York that summer to work; one a fashion stylist, the next a scientist, and the third the editor of a fanzine called *Cheap Date*. I visited them in July, in miniature dolls'-house apartments, totally enamored with the city's acerbic energy and there being a nail salon on every corner. After my public, weighty baptism by fire in England, disappearing into a simmering, anonymous city was bliss. I had been taken on by a famous old-school New York model agency, but bar that there was no other contingency plan, except grand designs to be in Tennessee Williams plays. The acting bit (and the fact that I was kind of rubbish) didn't come into the fantasy. I coveted the bosoms and upholstery of Elizabeth Taylor playing Maggie the Cat, lilies in my dressing room, which would be papered in chinoiserie, and a Richard Burton type proffering macaroons and love poems.

I know, I know. *Cringe*. I was young, though.

The thought of jumping into something with such abandon (and so little planning) now would cause me grave concern, but then it seemed as easy as pie. I simply rented out my house in England, bid goodbye to those at the Thai takeaway, bought a one-way ticket and left.

I moved into a friend's apartment on a tree-lined street in the West Village and our kitchen was the size of a runty flea. I'm ashamed to say not much cooking went on in it. I think he kept his dress shoes in the oven.

I arrived with a suitcase full of black clothes and no flat shoes. I thought in order to live in New York I should be teetering and faultless in black, a sort of walking Donna Karan advert. This was a big mistake – I crippled my feet, as I had a mortal, claustrophobic fear of the subway (since cured), and ended up walking blocks and blocks looking like a flustered, hobbling crow in evil-heeled open-toed stilettos. I eventually admitted defeat and hobbled as quickly as I could to the nearest Foot Locker to buy a pair of relieving flip-flops and a sensible pair of sneakers.

The hairdressers whose shop was downstairs from our apartment despaired at the sight of me leaving to go out at night without even a lick of lipstick.

"Just a quick dab of red?" they would say as I ran past. "What about an updo? Girl, you look a woebegone mess."

My new agency tried to have a *serious* talk with me. Would I like to be in the plus-size division, where, they assured me, I would become a rich thing and nab every cover of *Mode*? No, I demurred, I would not like to be in a division at all.

"But you are not thin enough to be in our women's division, and there is not enough of you to be one of our plus-size gals," they said.

"Well, I shall hover as a curvy question mark in no-man's-land, then, and if anyone wants to book me, they can book me," I replied. We had these conversations in an amazing Italian restaurant called Il Cantinori, a bowl of ribbolita dusted with Parmesan in my hands.

At castings, the other models and the clients were politely baffled. I sat in my black, next to girls polished like lean gymkhana ponies, all straight up and down, taut stomachs gleaming bronze in low-rise jeans, braless bee-sting breasts

New York was a brilliant place to be young and curious

just a suggestion through strappy T-shirts. The clients were polite on the whole, but they regarded me as though I was a curiosity landed in their midst, flicking through my portfolio with only a cursory interest.

Neither one thing nor the other, it seemed; I could not get a job for the life of me.

But I was discovering the city; its hidden corners, the winding walk up the East River, the Brooklyn Botanical Gardens (which helped when I was homesick) and the Tea and Sympathy restaurant on Greenwich Avenue (which provided just that).

I was enthralled by the take-out system in New York, where you could order, by phone, cuisine from any part of the world, and within fifteen minutes it would be winging its way to your doorstep: Japanese, Moroccan, Ethiopian, Indian, pizza that could break your heart. Such instant gratification, and very dangerous for an inquisitive glutton; but still I was walking everywhere, pounding the sidewalk with intent.

The thing I love about New York is that you can utterly lose yourself there amidst the clamoring sea of people. It is a transient place with a constant new turnover of creativity, youth and beauty. It was a brilliant place to be young and curious. I moved there in the days before the now ubiquitous bottle service in nightclubs and bars, where the only way to get a table is to order wine by the bottle. Back then money wasn't the thing that got you into a club. You could find yourself on any given Indian-summer night in some dive bar, sitting next to a beautiful poet, a movie star, a monosyllabic artist, a musician, an Andy Warhol creation or the girl on the cover of that month's *Vogue*. It was this unbridled spontaneity that made the city fun; the sense that absolutely anything could happen, if you just let it.

I was invited one night in November to a posh Madison Avenue party for a designer. I wore black. This time it was in my favor. The DJ was playing old-fashioned dirty rock and roll: the Ramones, the Stones, the Clash. I was dancing with a group of androgynous pretty boys, spinning around, and it was one of those nights where some magic is at play, and everything is kissed with fun and rightness.

"Have you met Steven Meisel?" The dream-girl makeup

artist, Pat McGrath, whom I knew from those early days in London, was tapping my arm.

"No," I said.

"Well, he's over there, and would like to meet you."

The word *icon* is bandied around in fashion, but Steven Meisel is the real deal. He is an extraordinary photographer, responsible for some of the most memorable images taken in the last twenty years. His work is constantly shifting shape and evolving, never tired. The shoots that he did in the early nineties with Linda Evangelista, Kate Moss, Naomi Campbell and Christy Turlington defined the zeitgeist of that decade, and created superstars in the process. Eighteen years on, he is still turning out the sort of work that makes other people wonder why they even bothered. His Italian *Vogue* covers are works of art in themselves, and represent a turning point in the career of the girl they feature. Here he was, with long black hair and a beautiful, impassive face.

"Hello," he said.

We chatted very briefly, and I went back to my dancing. "Well, that was interesting," I thought. It just seemed an apropos passing lovely moment, in a night full of them.

A few days later my agency called me in a froth of excitement.

"You've been booked to go to India, for *W* magazine just before Christmas, shooting in Goa with Tim Walker."

I thought about what I was going to eat for breakfast in India and became excruciatingly excited.

Tim Walker was another blessing, a completely original, kind, brilliant Englishman. His shoots begin with his notebooks, which are like diving into *Alice in Wonderland*. In these notebooks the seedlings of the shoot lie. He photographs everything with a whimsy and magic that for me is what fashion should be: fantastical, curious, irreverent and fun, with a course of elegance and beauty flowing through it.

We were in India for ten days. We ate ourselves silly; dosas, lassis, coconut milk curries. It was heady and exciting, shooting in fields of marigolds and crumbling marble-floored palaces in Goa, dancing in clouds of tulle through empty, echoing ballrooms filled with hot pink balloons. Posing like a

Vargas girl in a scarlet Norma Kamali swimsuit on the beach at sunset, followed by a glass of the powerful local hooch which made your throat burn to hell and tears stream down your face.

The day before we left to go back to New York, I was called to the front desk of the hotel, where the one phone resided. My booker's joy was all the more magnified in the transatlantic echo.

"Steven Meisel just booked you for an Italian *Vogue* cover!"

I spent the Christmas holidays cooking up a storm, the new millennium happily on my own, walking along a barren windswept beach in Martha's Vineyard. We shot the Italian *Vogue* story in the first week of January at a hip-hop club in New York's Chelsea. It was movie-star glamour at its finest: sumptuous jewel-colored turbans and peacock-feather eyes. The clothes fit perfectly. I think in retrospect they had all been made for me, as a sample size I was not.

I am forever grateful for this incarnation of my career, and to the people I had the luxury of working with. There was no fuss, no statement or apology made for my shape. The teams I worked with then – the photographers, stylists, makeup artists, hairdressers and manicurists – were utterly celebratory.

I was allowed, very simply, to just be. It was a wonderful education; in travel and adventure, diplomacy and grace. I was treated with great courtesy and warmth, and on the rare occasion I wasn't, I realized that I didn't have to work with that person again. The artistry and creativity I was lucky enough to be exposed to was splendid and limitless. In turn, it filled me brimful with confidence and curiosity. It is so easy to be dismissive or damning of modeling, and while it can be a supremely tricky path to navigate, I would not replace the experience I had for all the tea in China.

In the year 2000, I was on and off a plane about three times a week. I loved that I could wake up in Paris, go to a bakery on the way to the airport and be serving up croissants for breakfast as the sun rose the morning after in New York. Leaving the city at nighttime, in that old familiar drive to JFK, the Gotham skyline shimmering like a comic book; by lunchtime the next day I could be seated in a secret stone

Cuba smells like the earth after it has rained

courtyard on the Amalfi Coast, eating burrata and earthy vine-ripened tomatoes.

It was a good thing customs didn't search my bags – they were heaving with food and condiments. I ate fresh bread, smeared with sea-urchin roe, smoky olive oil and lemon juice in Greece. In Mumbai, the finest rice pudding, scented with cardamom and rose water. There was a simple vegetable soup in Milan; I still remember its sweet, staid comfort. Coconut rundown in Jamaica, conch ceviche in Harbour Island; the places I visited are remembered and categorized into tastes and smells. Cuba smells like the earth after it has rained, raw gasoline and overripe fruit. The taste of it is plantain, rice and beans – impossible to find without the addition of pork rind – and bitter tea. America tastes like Tropicana orange juice, molasses and bagels. The East Coast smells of Downy laundry detergent and pretzels; the West of jasmine and baked wood.

As soon as I landed at home, all I wanted to do was cook. (I had moved out of the West Village apartment and into my own.) Cooking had nothing to do with ball gowns and bouquets; it was self-sustaining and always there. I spent the summer mostly in upstate New York, cooking plates of Swedish meatballs (which I left well alone) for friends. I'm still semivegetarian after twenty years; I eat fish, but no other meat (the hangover of a hippie childhood) but am happy to cook organic free-range chicken, beef or lamb as long as I know where it came from. I draw the line at veal and *foie gras*; I can't see the need for such abject cruelty.

That summer I also bought an army of Le Creuset pots that I have to this day, a brilliant KitchenAid cake mixer and a blowtorch so I could scorch my own crème brûlée. I cooked my generous plates and rode a sweet, slow mare through the woods near Woodstock, thick with mosquitoes. I had yet to fully rediscover exercise, but all the to-ing and fro-ing was keeping me reasonably trim. I've always had a tendency to eat when I don't have enough to do or when I get bored, and am quite happy to mindlessly visit the freezer, sticking a spoon into ice cream every ten minutes. I did that too, and my weight could happily go up and down accordingly. I realized a freezer full of sorbet was the best preventative option, as I could power through an entire container of Il Laboratorio dark chocolate gelato in about thirty minutes.

Going full circle, it was spring, but maybe a year or two later, when I broke up with my first proper grown-up boyfriend and did all of the things that you often do when you break up with your boyfriend: I smoked a hundred cigarettes, cried till my eyes were raw and lost fifteen neurotic pounds. Some people get fat when they're miserable; certainly this was true of my teenage self, but as an adult, deliver me a week of extreme stress or misery and watch me disappear. I can't eat at all when I get sad; all I want is soup and easy-to-swallow baby food and, of all things, jelly beans. I love jelly beans when I'm sad. There's something about those primary-colored mushy balls of sugar that I can't get enough of. Luckily I don't often get sad; otherwise life would be very bleak and I would have no teeth left in my head.

After breaking up with the boyfriend, I did that other classic break-up thing; I hit the gym because I wanted to be much sexier than him. I did boxing with Public Enemy raging in the background. I did Pilates, I did yoga. I loved and continue to love yoga. I love the practicality of it; the awareness one has to have of both the breath and each and every muscle in the body. I hate trendy show-off yoga, where perfect coiffeured people who pretend to be peaceful are in mad hostile competition with one another over who can execute a brilliant cobra pose or wrap their ankles round their neck the quickest. I also don't get a certain kind of sweating yoga, where the room is heated to a zillion degrees and everyone's sweat pours on top of you as you contemplate the universe and the fact that you're in a human Petri dish of germs. A bit grim and unsanitary, I feel.

Practicing yoga made me calmer and leaner. Through yoga I started investigating alternative medicines and ways of eating: macrobiotics, which I still think is principally great, but maybe a bit complex to incorporate into your everyday life, and juice fasting, about which I feel the same thing.

My alternative period, which happened somewhere around

2004, also featured a flirtation with raw foodism, which was the cause of great mirth among my friends.

Still living in Manhattan, I found myself in the office of an unusual doctor – a man evangelical in his preaching on the benefits of a raw food diet – because of a friend who'd become a zealous raw foodist. The raw food doctor was oddly fascinating; he held my wrist and told me what year my tonsils had been removed, and named all the minor ailments I suffered. He was bang on. He continued to be bang on, until he whispered a suggestion that had something to do with the health benefits of drinking my own pee.

"Please don't continue!" I said. "I draw the line."

"Yes, some people are a bit funny about that one." He blushed.

Other than the pee-drinking (*why?! why?!*) I attached myself barnaclelike to his doctrine, annoying my friends and long-suffering then boyfriend with my reticence towards going out for dinner and refusals of cups of tea proffered with love. The raw food doctor told me that my friends might try to sabotage my new lifestyle, and he was dead right. I tried to ply them with Irish moss mousse and a hijiki sea vegetable casserole and I was greeted with shrieks of disgust. I filled the fridge with nut milk. My then boyfriend was allergic to nuts. His eyes accused me of treachery whenever he reached for a Diet Coke.

When I get sad, all I want are jelly beans

On my raw food diet, my skin shone bright like a gilded deity and my eyes glowed in a somewhat unearthly manner. My hips and bottom, however, swelled at an alarming rate, and I began to strongly resemble a pear. Picasso would have mistaken me for a fruit and painted me, so round and abundant was I. A pear with slightly strained clothes, a pear suffused with anguish, yet all the same, I was a pear with bloody good skin. I didn't care about my skin. I was seriously distressed.

"I just don't understand it." The good doctor and I sat in his grubby office on low chairs.

I patted my ample haunch woefully. "I thought that all of this was meant to be good for me. *And not fattening*; you said it wasn't fattening." I narrowed my eyes at him.

"Just how much exactly have you been eating?" he asked, pen delicately poised.

I decided to seek absolution with confession. I told him of

the deliciousness contained within the creamy folds of raw mock cheesecake, velvet slabs of raw mock chocolate and voluptuous blancmange, pure and raw. I wanted to share the joy I took in great silken smoothies made from nut milk, cups of raw honey and a plethora of exotic Amazonian berries, colored like the rainbow.

Under a blanket of virtue I had consumed raw food in spades, wantonly pretending that epic amounts of nuts and avocados doused in honey with dates on top were "good for me" just as long as *it was all raw*.

The doctor looked dismayed by my confession, as if I had let him down. Sighing, he lowered his voice conspiratorially, as if to deliver a piece of indispensable wisdom.

"Innkeepers are gluttons," he began. "Lawyers are gluttons. Indeed, most doctors are gluttons; yes, they are."

There was a heavy silence. My eyes widened. His next sentence was sharp like a butcher's knife.

"Spiritual people are not gluttons. They are simply not that interested in food."

Feeling like a greedy, unspiritual deviant, I paid him $200 and walked home to a fridge that was groaning with fattening, raw, murderous-to-my-boyfriend food. I smoked a cigarette and had a very unraw cup of coffee that shot quickly to my brain like an injection of adrenaline.

My raw adventure was short-lived, much to the relief of those I knew

My raw adventure was short-lived, much to the relief of those I knew. It was incredibly time-consuming and the people at the raw food takeaway took an hour to make one smoothie. They floated, unmoored, and moved as if wading through quicksand. I decided a plate of mashed potatoes might keep them on the ball and ground them a bit. It took them ten minutes to answer a question. It made me feel rageful. My brother liked to go there with me, just to watch me get annoyed as strangers tried to feel my chakras and my smoothie sat gathering dust because the person who was making it forgot about it and wandered slowly off in search of some nuts to grind.

I had to concede that I was just not that patient; I was gluttonous and proud, and that's all there was to it. My brother still misses the Irish moss mousse.

The raw food thing began because of something that

had happened in India the year before. Having been the same shape for a good few years, I went to India to make a film in 2003. As I said before, I am now adept at lip-synching in Hindi while dancing with bells on my feet (which may perhaps be useful one day); but above and beyond that, it was a somewhat unfortunate experience. But oh, oh, oh, the masala chai at teatime, the syrupy sweet rasmalai, the crispy dosas. The dinners at people's houses comprised of so many perfect things: the saffron rice just so with slivers of almonds and cardamom, the uttapam pancakes for breakfast with tomato gravy.

I had been to India many times, and I had never been ill, but in the last week of being there, I was. It could have happened anywhere. I flew to London where I was mis-diagnosed, and as a result of being on incorrect antibiotics I got sicker. I got very thin, very quickly. Having been on a course of knockout antibiotics for three months, I then got a deeply nasty bacterial infection named *C. difficile*, common in people with compromised immune systems who have been on long-term courses of antibiotics, which was infinitely worse than the initial thing. Oddly enough, the only thing that cures it is the thing that causes it – more antibiotics. I looked and felt like a ghost (although my love for Indian food was not remotely challenged by the illness; if anything, the moment I was better, it came back with even more verve than before).

Sitting in the back of a cab in London, I'd get the "I much preferred you when you were fat" train of conversation.

"Yes, I know, I know, I much preferred me when I was fat too; now, could you please take me to Waterloo?"

I did not feel sexy when I was that skinny. I felt tired and grisly, unfeminine and awful. It took about a year and a half to get back on track (my brief excursion into raw foodism notwithstanding), and I had to be militant about what I ate. I had been told by the doctor to avoid dairy, sugar, and wheat at that time, all possible aggravators of a challenged, war-torn stomach. If anything positive came out of it, it was that I slowed down, and learned to cook within the bounds of what I could eat without causing a return flare-up.

I made delicious rice puddings with lemon zest and rice

milk, replacing the sugar with agave nectar, a low-glycemic syrup (suitable for diabetics) that comes from a cactus plant and has the mellow taste of honey. I would eat this rice pudding cold for breakfast. I ate a lot of gentle foods – soups and stews, mashed sweet potatoes, puréed apples with cinnamon, slow-cooked porridge.

What that nasty few intense months of sickness offered me was a chance to stop leaping around like a jumping bean, to see food not just as sustenance, but also as medicine, and to truly follow a course of balance. I couldn't overeat, skip a meal, or go without sleep. If I did, I would be riddled with stomach pain, faint, or catch any bug that was going. In some odd way, dreaded as it was, I learned a lot from beginning to end. I stopped being faddish and casual with my body. I felt intensely grateful for its health. I incorporated all of the things I learned along the way, and rather than using one extreme, merged little parts of each of them with what I felt worked for me into a practical daily routine.

This could mean a juice on waking, made from ginger, pear and apple, and oatmeal with rice milk and some chopped banana a few hours later. Lunch could be a simple puréed vegetable soup, or possibly a salad with hard-boiled eggs and sheep's feta. Supper would be fish with some brown rice and vegetables. Exercise would be gentle yoga before work, or a walk after. In this way, I got my health and body into a calm rhythm.

And really, that's the thing, the rhythm. You don't need to be ill to find one. Think of a child's routine. You wouldn't send a child off to school without breakfast; you wouldn't tell him to have a Diet Coke and a protein bar for lunch because you didn't have time. You wouldn't feed that child a plate groaning with nothing but high-fat protein and tell him he couldn't eat any carbs or fruit. No, you would feed him a balanced breakfast; you would make sure he had a packed lunch, with an apple or a banana for good measure. In the evening, for dinner, whatever the amount of protein, he would have some starch. He would have treats. You wouldn't pinch his flesh and tell him he was fat, and that if only he lost ten pounds he would be more appealing. Regardless of whether the child in question was obese or of average weight, you would be tolerant, kind and nurturing, providing the most comprehensive nourishment you could muster in order to give him a healthy existence. Why are you any different?

Gradually throughout those years in New York I had whittled myself down, purely through being sensible and exercising. There was no great pound-shedding all at once (apart from the India experience). It was slow and quiet, and I didn't really notice, though other people did. From 2001 onward, I had a certain routine. I did yoga three times a week, I avoided processed food, and if I ate bread, it was good whole-grain bread. I learned to read labels, but not obsessively. And in doing so, I gradually developed more of an understanding of what I was putting in my body.

I made delicious rice puddings with lemon zest and rice milk

I devised a simple mental checklist so that I ate in a manner that was balanced and aware. It is now second nature to me:

Hidden sugar

There is a lot of hidden sugar in things that you wouldn't assume have sugar. Some soy milk is loaded with cane sugar, as soy is not naturally sweet. Better to use a brand that has no sugar or one that is sweetened with brown rice syrup or fruit juice.

The myth of low-calorie/low-fat

The same is true of a lot of low-fat/low-calorie products, as food manufacturers traditionally make up for the deficit of fat and calories (and taste) with sugar, which leaves you with an insulin spike, and wanting more and more still.

Craving something sweet

I think it's far better to have some quality high-cacao dark chocolate, or a small bowl of good ice cream (one without corn syrup and a busload of weird additives) than an entire packet of low-calorie biscuits. The chocolate tends to satiate that craving, whereas a poor alternative will just leave you hungering for more. A small bowl of good, rich, dense vanilla or chocolate ice cream or gelato will greet a sugar craving admirably. A massive bowl of light-as-a-feather low-fat ice cream, crammed with chemical binders and high-fructose corn syrup, will do nothing but give you a bellyache and have you longing for sweetness an hour later.

Wholesome bread

Still in my pajamas, I made a sort of fantasy Viking feast

The same goes for bready things, and you can tell quality by simply picking it up in your hands. The weightier a bread product is, the higher the concentration of whole grains and good stuff in it, as a rule. A piece of poor-quality heavily processed bread will feel as if it could float away like a dandelion, but will have the opposite effect on your body. Once you learn this, it's an easy science.

Considered alcohol

Diet books will tell you to lay off alcohol if you have weight to lose, as alcohol is filled with empty calories. One glass of something won't hurt. Copious glasses of spirits mixed with sugary fizzy drinks or juice won't help the cause. Have one glass of wine, or vodka with fresh lime and soda.

By the end of 2004 I was finally on a happy even keel, and that year culminated in one of the sweetest Christmases ever. My mum and my brother and sister, Clover and Luke, came to New York, and we decided to make the day rather decadent, and about very late breakfast rather than lunch. We played brilliant naff Christmas music, and, still in my pajamas, I made a sort of fantasy Viking feast: fruit compote, Swiss muesli, frittata, smoked fish on thick rye bread with crème fraîche and capers. I think I made a flourless chocolate cake as well. I know we ate a lot.

It was just the four of us; our breakfast stretched on until about 4:00 p.m., and then we went for a walk in the snow. I saw them all again the following April. The snowdrops had by then come out to play.

spring
breakfasts

Grilled papaya with lime

SERVES 1–2
1 large ripe papaya
Zest and juice of
  2 juicy limes, plus
  extra juice to serve

I ate this in the Caribbean island of Nevis with no one but a greedy bird for company. He wolfed the lot.

Preheat the broiler. Cut the papaya in half, scoop out the seeds and throw them away. Squeeze the lime juice into the hollows and add a little zest on the top. Put under the broiler for a few minutes until seared on the top. Squeeze more lime juice on to taste.

serve with some good
toast and a saucy smile

Coquette's eggs

SERVES 2

4 eggs

Salt and pepper

Olive oil

Roasted red peppers –
I lazily use a jar of
Italian sweet char-
grilled peppers, but
obviously you can
make them yourself
too. (Chop some red
peppers, baste them
with olive oil and
blast them under the
broiler for a few
minutes.)

A good chunk of feta
cheese, crumbled

A handful of fresh
basil leaves, chopped

When my boyfriend and I were courting, he came over for brunch and this is what I cooked, albeit rather nervously . . . the name is somewhat bolder than I felt that day, but something obviously worked; fate or cooking, we'll never know.

The trick to good scrambled eggs is a very low heat and fresh eggs. Whisk the eggs in a bowl, and add salt and pepper. In a pan, gently heat some olive oil. Pour in the eggs, stirring continuously or you'll have an omelette on your hands. I leave the pan on the burner for only about 1 minute, if that, after which I take it off and the eggs cook themselves, like magic. It depends how well done you like them, really. I abhor runny scrambled eggs.

In a separate pan, heat the peppers and crumble in the feta. This should take a minute or two. Pour on top of the eggs, mix it in gently, season and put some chopped basil on top. Serve with some good toast and a saucy smile.

Swiss muesli

Swiss muesli basically sucks up anything in its path. What begins as a rather dry, mean-looking thing is by morning plump and full of promise.

Grate the apples coarsely and put in a medium-sized mixing bowl. Pour the lemon juice on top – this stops them browning and adds a welcome degree of tartness to the proceedings.

Mix all the other ingredients in and stir with a wooden spoon. I leave it covered overnight in the fridge, so the fruit is plump and swollen and the oats have absorbed the yogurt, and have it next day for breakfast with some more yogurt and a drizzle of honey or syrup.

SERVES 2 AND ENOUGH TO SAVE

4 apples, peeled and cored
2 tablespoons of lemon juice
2 cups of rolled oats
2 cups of plain yogurt, plus extra to serve
½ cup of raisins
½ cup of raspberries
¼ cup of chopped walnuts
Honey, agave syrup or maple syrup, to serve

Scrambled tofu with pesto and spinach

SERVES 2

For the pesto
4 cups of fresh basil
  leaves
1 cup of olive oil
½ cup of pine nuts
1 large clove of garlic,
  peeled and crushed
½ cup of freshly grated
  Parmesan
Salt and pepper

1 tablespoon of olive
  oil
2 cups of semifirm
  tofu, crumbled
1 cup of baby spinach
  leaves

Pesto in all its green garlicky glory is a love song to the spring. The smell of wild garlic is one I associate with childhood and spring because the woods in Buckinghamshire were full of its piquant sting; that, and swathes of bluebells.

First, make the pesto. Put the basil, olive oil, pine nuts and garlic in a blender and pulse on medium. Transfer to a bowl and stir in the Parmesan. Taste and season accordingly.

On a low heat, put the 1 tablespoon of olive oil into a pan and pour in your crumbled tofu. Add the spinach and stir until the spinach has wilted – a minute or two.

Pour the pesto over the tofu and spinach mix (you probably won't need it all; you can put the leftovers in a jam jar and keep it in the fridge for when you want it). Mix it all together, until everything is hot and the tofu's stained green.

NOTE:
Pesto is traditionally made painstakingly in a pestle and mortar. I honestly think it is just as good made in the blender or food processor, and a hell of a lot easier if you're in a hurry.

Lemon and ricotta spelt pancakes

Hurrah for the happy, zesty, springlike combination of lemon and cheese!

In a large mixing bowl, combine the ricotta cheese, milk and egg yolks. Stir in the flour and baking powder and stir until you have a batter. (There is no need to sift the flour as it gets rid of all the good bran bits and the mixture is light enough anyway.)

In a separate bowl, whisk the egg whites until white and foamy, but not stiff, and fold them into the first bowl. Add the lemon zest and agave or maple syrup and stir.

In a large frying pan, heat the oil, and drop in small dollops of batter, about the size of a large chocolate coin. Cook the pancakes for a minute or two on each side; you want them to be a sort of honeyed brown.

Serve with some raspberries, and a little more agave or maple syrup.

NOTE:
The batter is very light and fluffy, so it's important to make only very small pancakes, otherwise they are almost impossible to turn over without breaking up. The mixture makes enough for four people and has to be used at the time of making. Quantities can be easily halved to serve two.

SERVES 4 (MAKES ABOUT 20 SMALL PANCAKES)

1 cup of soft ricotta cheese
½ cup of 2% milk
2 large eggs, separated
½ cup of spelt flour
1 teaspoon of baking powder
2 teaspoons of finely grated lemon zest
1 tablespoon of agave or maple syrup, plus extra to serve
2 teaspoons of sunflower oil

Grilled figs with ricotta and thyme honey

SERVES 2

6 figs, quartered but still attached at the bottom

Tiny dot of unsalted butter

1 tablespoon of thyme or other aromatic honey

2 slices of ricotta

My brother Luke is obsessed with both honey and cheese. He once called me to tell me of a dream he'd had in which he ate the ham from a pig that had been reared solely on a diet of honey and ricotta. "It was the most delicious ham I've ever eaten," he said. "And when I woke up I felt very depressed, because it was just a dream." My family. Gluttons in sleep too.

Preheat the broiler. Wash the figs and carefully cut them open – score them twice. Dot each one with a mini amount of butter and do the same with the honey – just a quick drizzle on each one, not a monsoon cloud.

Put them on a cookie sheet under a searing broiler for 2 minutes. Serve with a slice of ricotta, draped with another dignified slip of honey.

Rhubarb compote with orange-flower yogurt and pistachios

You may need to buy forced rhubarb if you are desirous of utter wanton swirls of pink. If you are not, it might be more of a pedestrian green, which is OK too.

In a saucepan on a low heat, stew the rhubarb with ½ cup of agave syrup or honey and the orange juice until it has reduced and thickened. This should take about 4 minutes. Cool.

Mix the yogurt with the orange-flower water and a teaspoon of agave syrup or honey in a bowl.

Pour the cooled rhubarb on top and sprinkle with the pistachios.

SERVES 2

4 medium-sized stalks of rhubarb, chopped into ½-inch pieces

½ cup plus 1 teaspoon of agave syrup or honey

½ cup of orange juice

2 cups of low-fat Greek yogurt (or however much you like)

1 teaspoon of orange-flower water

A handful of unsalted slivered pistachio nuts

spring
lunches

My mama's baked acorn squash

SERVES 4

5 acorn squash – baseball-sized
16oz bag of frozen petite peas
2 tablespoons of olive oil
A handful of fresh mint, finely chopped
1 tablespoon of light brown sugar
Salt and pepper
Feta cheese, to serve (optional)

I was staying with my mum one weekend while there was a storm raging and very little in the fridge. This is what she made, and it was characteristically delicious.

Preheat the oven to 350°F. Cut the squash in half and remove the seeds. Put the squash cut side down in a baking pan in 1½ inches of salted water. Cook in the oven for about 1 hour or until tender.

Cook the frozen peas as usual, drain and add the olive oil, the finely chopped mint and a spoonful of brown sugar. Remove the squash from the oven, turn them over and fill with the pea mixture. Season to taste. You could also crumble some feta cheese on top.

Crab and fennel salad

I grew up crabbing in Massachusetts, where my maternal granny lives. One of the best meals I've ever eaten was a boiled lobster on the beach there, served with some melted butter, a corn on the cob and an ice-cold beer. Inspired by those *al fresco* beachy lunches, I came up with this pretty spring salad using crab instead. A note on crabs and lobsters – if you can't stomach cooking them, you shouldn't really be eating them.

Mix the crabmeat, mayonnaise and lemon juice together in a bowl.

Wash the fennel and cut off the tops and excess stalks. Trim the bottom of the bulb and get rid of any of the outer leaves if they are tough or discolored. Cut the bulb in half and slice lengthwise with a sharp knife, as thinly as possible, from the root to the top of the bulb.

Mix the vinaigrette ingredients in a small bowl with a fork. Put a handful of frisée on two plates, top with a generous dollop of the crab, and arrange the fennel in a circle around the crab. Dress the salad with some of the vinaigrette.

SERVES 2

Meat from 2 medium-sized cooked crabs
1 tablespoon of mayonnaise
1 teaspoon of lemon juice
1 large fennel bulb
A large handful of frisée

For the vinaigrette
2 tablespoons of white wine vinegar
6 tablespoons of good olive oil
Salt and pepper
1 teaspoon of Dijon mustard

inspired by *al fresco* beachy lunches

Teddy's lettuce soup

SERVES 2–3

2 heads of lettuce –
   garden or butter
   lettuce works best

2 cups of chicken or
   vegetable stock

1 cup of frozen peas

2 cups of 2% milk

1 teaspoon of light
   brown sugar

1 pinch of freshly
   grated nutmeg

Salt and pepper

Crème fraîche or a pat
   of butter, to serve

My mum, Tessa, has been called Teddy since she was little. She trained at the French Culinary Institute and can cook (or rescue) any dish. (She also rescues animals with the same alacrity and currently has five dogs, five cats and two canaries, named after her ex-husbands.)

Cut the lettuces into thin ribbons after giving them a thorough wash and discarding any tough leaves. Keep those for your tortoise. Put the lettuces in a pan with just enough stock to cover and gently simmer on a low heat, keeping a vigilant eye on them – there are few things nastier than charred, acrid lettuce!

Keep simmering and adding the stock until the greens are soft. Add the peas and cook for another 4 minutes or so. Take off the heat, cool for a minute or two, then purée with care.

Return to the pan and, on a low heat, gently add the milk – less for a thicker soup, more for a lighter summery soup. Add the brown sugar, a pinch of nutmeg, and salt and pepper to taste.

If you are going to chill the soup, put it in the fridge, adding a teaspoon of crème fraîche to each bowl prior to serving. If eating hot, dot a tiny bit of butter on the top instead.

Asparagus soup with Parmesan

SERVES 4–6
2 leeks, white parts
   only
1 shallot
1 small bunch of
   asparagus (about
   24 small to
   medium stems)
Olive oil
1 quart of hot stock
   – vegetable or
   chicken
Parmesan rind
Salt and pepper

I preface this with a cautionary tale.

I was happily trying out this soup at home to give you reasonable measurements. I was on my own, late at night, listening to a questionable song, and all was going well. That is, until I put the still rather hot soup in the blender to purée it. As I pressed the purée function, my power shorted. And as my power shorted, the soup decided to geyser from the blender, covering me, the floors and wall in a thick slick of green. I shouted "F***!" at the top of my voice, but also laughed.

I tried to work out whether the blender was malfunctioning or whether the power had gone, and deduced that the intelligent way to divine this was by checking the washing machine, which had been on. (The fuse box was fine.) I clumped over to the washing machine – feet dotted with leeks – and opened the door. A great swoosh of cold soapy water cascaded over me, and the green floor.

"F***!" I shouted again, hopping on one leg, trying to stem the flow. Then I cried. This got me nowhere, and didn't bring the power back. Fridge, oven, phone and computer were down – not a help when one is writing a cookbook. My mobile had one bar of power but gets no reception in my house. I stood in the only corner of the garden where it does work, trying to get hold of an emergency electrician.

At 11:30 p.m. the electrician came. He looked at my green-crusted sweater and tear-stained face with distaste. He gently massaged the fuse box. Everything came roaring back to life.

"Switch tripped," he said. "It's all fine; probably the blender."

"It was *not* the blender," I said defensively. "It's a lovely blender."

He raised an eyebrow and left. I sat on the floor and ate the scant remains out of the blender with a big spoon. The soup was good. I laughed.

Chop the leeks and shallot finely. Chop the asparagus, minus the tough ends (you can keep them for stock later, if you feel like a domestic goddess).

In a soup pot, heat 1 tablespoon or so of olive oil and gently sweat the leeks and shallots until they turn translucent. Add the hot stock and the Parmesan rind. Leave this for 15 minutes or so on a low heat and pop the asparagus in at the end, for about 7 minutes. Season; remove the Parmesan rind (what's left of it) with a spoon. Let the soup cool a bit and then either purée it or leave it as a broth with vegetables. Both, as I know, work.

Zucchini and watercress soup

SERVES 2
2 zucchini
2 handfuls of
　watercress
1 small onion, finely
　chopped
Olive oil
1 quart of chicken or
　vegetable stock
Salt and pepper
1 tablespoon of light
　cream
1 pinch of saffron
　strands (optional)

Easy as pie, deeply good for you and green as the grass. My spring lunches seem to have a definite green theme.

Wash and roughly chop the zucchini and watercress.

In a heavy-bottomed soup pan, sauté the onion in a little olive oil until translucent. Add the zucchini and stock and cook on a low heat for 10 minutes. Add the watercress and cook for another 5 minutes. Season.

Let the soup stand for a while to cool, then transfer to a blender and purée. Once puréed, return to the pot, warm and add the cream. You could also add a pinch of saffron. Serve with a dash of olive oil.

Baby vegetable fricassee

This is a pretty gem of a dish, tender and perfectly formed.

Heat the olive oil in a large pan. Add the onion, garlic and leeks and sauté on low for 5 minutes, adding a little stock if it gets too dry. Add the rest of the vegetables and the bay leaf and cook on low for another 4 minutes. Cover and cook for another 10 minutes.

Meanwhile, in another pan, melt the butter and gently add the arrowroot, whisking for 1 minute. Slowly add the stock, whisking it in so it doesn't get lumpy and vile. Add the vegetables and simmer for a few minutes. Season, remove the bay leaf unless you don't mind a mouthful of it and eat.

SERVES 2

2 tablespoons of olive oil
½ cup of roughly chopped onion
1 clove of garlic, peeled and finely chopped
4 baby leeks, halved or quartered
1½ cups of vegetable stock
10 ears baby corn, halved
6 baby zucchini, halved
6 baby carrots, halved
A handful of snow peas
1 bay leaf
Salt and pepper

For the roux
1 large tablespoon of butter
1½ tablespoons of arrowroot

Fava bean salad with pecorino and asparagus

SERVES 2

1 cup of baby
   asparagus tips
1 cup of cooked fresh
   or frozen baby Fava
   (broad) beans, skins
   removed (If fresh,
   they will need to be
   blanched to remove
   the skins. You can
   also use the same
   amount of drained
   and rinsed canned
   beans.)
A small handful of
   fresh mint, finely
   chopped
3 tablespoons of good-
   quality olive oil
Salt and pepper
½ cup of pecorino
   cheese, shaved

I had something similar to this in a very good Italian restaurant in New York. It is a simple pleasure, perfect with a little sea salt and a rich musky dollop of olive oil.

Put the asparagus in a pan of boiling salted water and boil for 2–3 minutes. Drain and rinse under cold water.

Place the beans and asparagus tips in a small salad bowl and add the mint. Pour on the olive oil and add some salt and pepper. Add the cheese. Eat in a balmy garden with a few fat blowsy bumblebees nearby, but not close enough to harass you.

spring
suppers

served in the garden, surrounded by love

Sea bass with black olive salsa and baby zucchini

SERVES 2
2 sea bass fillets
Olive oil
Juice of 1 lemon
Salt and pepper
6 baby zucchini, halved

For the black olive salsa
1 cup of pitted black
   olives
1 cup of cherry
   tomatoes, halved
A handful of chopped
   fresh basil and dill
Juice of 1 lemon
½ a red chile, deseeded
   and chopped
¼ cup of olive oil
1 lemon, sliced, rind
   and pith removed,
   to garnish

This would be a good date dinner. On my thirtieth birthday I had sea bass cooked for me and served in the garden, surrounded by twinkling candles and a whole lot of love.

Preheat the oven to 375°F. Marinate the bass in a mixture of olive oil, lemon juice and salt and pepper for about 20 minutes.

In a mixing bowl, mix the olives, tomatoes, chopped basil and dill, lemon juice, red chile and olive oil. Set aside.

Slice the zucchini lengthwise, season and splash with olive oil, then bake in the oven for 20 minutes.

Pan-fry the bass in some hot olive oil, cooking it for 2 minutes on each side. Add the bass to the plates and top with the black olive salsa, serving the baby zucchini on the side, sprinkled with extra dill and lemon slices.

Pan-fried orange halibut with watercress purée

This came about after experimenting with spring flavors – the ingredients make for happy pan-fellows. Halibut is one of my favorite fishes to cook with because it's so meaty and steaklike. The mixture of orange, watercress and herbs creates a light, fresh and fragrant supper.

First, make the watercress purée. Discard the watercress stems and finely chop the leaves. On a low heat, melt the butter, add the watercress and cook until it is soft, which should take a few minutes. Take it off the heat and either blend it, or pass it through a food mill. Season to taste and keep warm.

In a very, very hot nonstick pan, fry the halibut steaks for a few minutes on each side. When they are getting crispy and brown, add a little olive oil and the orange juice and zest to the pan and cook for another minute. Serve on top of the watercress purée with chopped herbs, if you have them on hand: parsley, tarragon or chives would all be good.

SERVES 2

For the watercress purée
1 large bunch of
    watercress
1 tablespoon of butter
Salt and pepper

2 thick halibut steaks
1 glug of olive oil
Juice and zest of ½ an
    orange
Fresh chopped herbs –
    ideally parsley,
    tarragon or chives,
    to serve (optional)

Hortense's fish soup

Hortense Ramos is a gifted cook from Portugal whom I was lucky enough to get to know when I lived in America. Her baking is unparalleled, and her lemon bars could make grown men weep. This is a recipe that she kindly passed on to me.

First, cut the fish into ½-inch cubes and shell and devein the shrimp. Cut the scallops into quarters, scrub and debeard the mussels and set them all aside.

Heat the oil in a large heavy-bottomed pan and add the onions, leeks, celery and green pepper. Keep on a low heat and stir continuously, until the onions are translucent. Stir in the cayenne and salt and pepper to taste. Add the wine and chopped tomatoes, cooking for about 5 minutes or so, then add the fish stock, in its entirety, and cook for another 20 minutes.

Add the monkfish or bass and cook for about 2 minutes, then add the shrimp, scallops and mussels. Stirring often, continue cooking for about 3 minutes, or until the mussels have opened. (Discard any mussels that don't open.) Stir in the Pernod or Ricard and season to taste. Ladle into bowls and serve with a big green salad on the side.

NOTE:
Fresh mussels should be healthy-looking, intact and tightly shut. Any that are slightly open and don't close when lightly tapped should be discarded.

SERVES 4 AS A HEARTY MAIN COURSE

1lb of white monkfish or striped bass
8oz of raw shrimp
8oz of sea scallops
12 mussels
¼ cup of olive oil
2 cups of finely chopped onions
2 cups of finely chopped leeks, white parts only
¾ cup (2 stalks) of finely chopped celery
1 large green bell pepper, deseeded and finely chopped
¼ teaspoon of cayenne pepper
Salt and pepper
½ cup of white wine
3 (14½oz) cans of chopped tomatoes
1 quart of fish stock
1 tablespoon of Pernod or Ricard

lamb in all its juicy, crusted glory

Crusted rack of lamb for Luke

SERVES 2

2 three-racks of lamb

Olive oil

1 egg white

2 tablespoons of ground almonds

1 clove of garlic, peeled and chopped

½ teaspoon of ground cumin

A handful of finely chopped fresh mint, parsley and cilantro

For the roasted sweet potatoes with rosemary

2 medium-sized sweet potatoes, peeled and cut into fat chunks

A scant handful of chopped fresh rosemary

2 tablespoons of olive oil

My brother Luke loves lamb, the bloodier the better. He was up in arms that I didn't have a lamb recipe in the book. So although I don't eat lamb, this is for him in all its juicy, crusted glory, and for all lamb-loving carnivores out there.

First, brown the lamb in a searing hot pan with a little bit of olive oil. You just want to seal the juices in, so brown it for literally just a few minutes.

Preheat the oven to 375°F. In a mixing bowl, whisk the egg white and add the ground almonds, garlic, cumin and herbs. Mix well and then pat on the loin side of the lamb, making sure it is properly covered.

You want to put the sweet potatoes in the oven about 25 minutes before the lamb, in a roasting pan, covered with the rosemary and some splashes of olive oil. When they have done their time, add the lamb to the oven in a separate pan next to the sweet potatoes and cook for 20 minutes, less if you like it really rare. The sweet potatoes should be ready at exactly the same time as the lamb if you time it like this.

Char-grilled scallops on pea purée

Make sure your pan is blisteringly hot, and don't, as my boyfriend does, call them "scalps."

Cook the peas in boiling water for 5 minutes. Drain and put in a blender with the butter or oil, the mint and crème fraîche. Purée, taste and season accordingly.

In a large skillet, heat the olive oil, add the scallops and let them brown on each side. When they are nearly there, throw in the lemon zest and chile and give them a toss.

Put the pea purée on two plates and serve the scallops on top.

SERVES 2

2 cups of frozen peas

1 tablespoon of butter or olive oil

1 tablespoon of chopped fresh mint

1 tablespoon of crème fraîche

Salt and pepper

1 tablespoon of olive oil

8 large scallops

2 teaspoons of lemon zest

1 teaspoon of dried red chile flakes

Turmeric tofu with cherry tomato quinoa pilaf

"What is quinoa?" people ask me. "It's an ancient grain," say I. It's a weird magic grain, gluten-free and protein-packed, and it cooks just like couscous. You can get it now in most supermarkets and certainly in a good health food shop.

Bring the water to the boil in a saucepan, add the quinoa, cover and simmer for 10–15 minutes. Leave to cool. Put the quinoa into a bowl and add a spoonful of olive oil. Add the chopped scallion, tomatoes and some of the chopped herbs.

In a skillet, heat some olive oil and sauté the tofu, giving it a liberal dash of turmeric so it goes an ambrosial golden color. You should cook it for a few minutes on each side.

Make the dressing by mixing the crème fraîche, lemon juice and a good teaspoon or two of lemon zest together. It will be very thick – this is what you want. Season it with lots of black pepper. Dress the quinoa salad and serve with the tofu on top and another handful of chopped herbs.

SERVES 2
2 cups of water
1 cup of quinoa
Olive oil
1 scallion, chopped
2 cups of cherry
  tomatoes, halved
A handful of fresh
  parsley, chopped
A handful of fresh
  cilantro, chopped
6 slices of firm tofu
A good sprinkle of
  ground turmeric

For the dressing
¼ cup of crème fraîche
Zest and juice of
  1 lemon
Black pepper

Chicken stew with green olives

SERVES 4

Olive oil

1 chicken, cut up by
   your butcher

2 cloves of garlic,
   peeled and crushed

1 fennel bulb, roughly
   chopped

1 cup of white wine

14½oz can of chopped
   tomatoes

1 cup of chicken stock

½ cup of green pitted
   olives

A scant handful of
   fresh basil, chopped

There's something about those plump green Italian olives that sings of spring. Plus this stew is very simple to make. A kitchen supper with the doors thrown open, accompanied by a good summery white wine, probably Pouilly-Fuissé.

In a large pan, heat 3 tablespoons of oil and add the chicken, cooking for 15 minutes, until it has browned. Remove from the pan and set aside.

In the same pan, sweat the garlic and fennel in a little more oil for a few minutes. Pour the wine over, add the tomatoes and cook for another 10 minutes on low. Put the chicken back in the pan and cook on low for around 30 minutes, adding the stock little by little. Put the olives and basil in at the end for a few minutes and serve.

Shrimp, avocado, grapefruit, watercress and pecan salad

Perfect for a lunch where the impression of effort is required, but where actual time spent is minimal.

Make a large pretty plate with the shrimp, avocado, grapefruit and watercress. Arrange however your heart desires.

Put all of your dressing ingredients in the blender and whiz for a minute or two.

Toast the pecans in a hot oven for a few minutes.

Pour the dressing on the salad and top with the pecans.

SERVES 2
2 cups of cooked
   shelled shrimp
1 avocado, pitted and
   sliced
1 grapefruit, peeled
   and segmented
1 bunch of watercress
½ cup of pecans

For the dressing
Juice of 3 limes
A big handful of fresh
   cilantro, finely
   chopped
A small handful of
   fresh mint, chopped
1 green chile, deseeded
   and chopped
1 teaspoon of sugar or
   honey
½ teaspoon of fish
   sauce

GRAPES and Bees.....

summer

BREAKFASTS
Cinnamon roast peaches with vanilla yogurt
Blueberry strawberry smoothie
Cold frittata with goat's cheese and zucchini
Scrambled eggs with watercress and smoked salmon
Breakfast burrito
Homemade muesli with strawberry yogurt

LUNCHES
Avocado soup
Quinoa salad with tahini dressing
Beet soup
Pea soup
Summer squash with tomato sauce and pine nuts
Salad niçoise sans anchovies and potatoes
Fish cakes

SUPPERS
Linguine with tomatoes, lemon, chile and crab
Warm ratatouille
Chicken and fennel au gratin
Coconut curry with shrimp
Grilled vegetables with halloumi cheese
Barbequed salmon on a cedar plank
Wild rice risotto

I moved back to England in the summer of 2007, a summer famous for its incessant rain. I fell into the sodden landscape of my homeland as if I were collapsing onto an old familiar feather bed. I moved to the country. There were no street lights, no take-out menus, no horns beeping, nothing; nothing but stillness, stars and raw green fields. I looked at my life spread before me in moving boxes and I made a bowl of porridge, eating it from my mother's old pansy-covered china as I sat on the empty floor wondering what was next.

There is not a tidy ending to this story, as life is ongoing and not always tidy. There are many things over which we have no control, but the day-to-day managing of our own bodies should not have to be part of that uncertainty. I suppose the question is: how can we incorporate a way of eating into our lives that is sensible, enjoyable, maintainable and practical? This is where my experience can hopefully be of some assistance.

The recipes here are all things I cook and eat. Nothing in the book requires hours of preparation; indeed, most are things that can be easily cooked after work, or made for everyone. As I mention throughout, I really don't believe in cutting out food groups or subscribing to militant, forbidding diets, so you will not find that here.

What I do believe in is moderation and balance, because both have served me well, and I try on a daily basis to let those two things be my guide.

I think that if we take the time to be conscious of the needs and wants of our own bodies, rather than permanently fixating on what's wrong with them, then the whole weight thing immediately becomes less of a struggle. That's why there are recipes here for rainy, insatiable chocolate days and lighter things for the gossamer, less hungry summer evenings.

Sometimes you may want just soup for lunch, at others a great bowl of pasta and maybe a lighter supper. I vacillate between the two, dipping in and out, not married to any particular thing. The options presented here are all part of that formula. If you can have faith in your own picking and choosing, then it is a simple equation. As much as we pretend we don't, we all have a good idea about what is good for us; the foods that make us feel energized, healthy and at our optimum best.

Sexy is having the energy to romp with your beloved

And please, don't be swayed or thwarted by some glossy fictional food diary that a stick-thin starlet swears she lives by, including her ten almonds or boring cup of cottage cheese for a snack. Yikes. Those things are often plucked from the ether or are dreamed up in the publicist's office. The joke is that right this instant the very same starlet that we read about and whose food diary we covet is sitting on a plane reading a magazine, wistfully thinking, "God, I really wish I looked like Gisele/Jessica Biel/Kate Hudson in a bikini. I wonder what she eats, who her nutritionist/trainer/surgeon is . . . I really must find out."

I *long* for a bottom like J Lo's but it is highly unlikely, even if I spend the rest of my days doing ten thousand lunges on rising. My lucky sister has that coveted bum, but she hates her legs. In the genetic draw I got the long legs, she got the bum. That's the way it goes. Maybe in my next life I can inherit that splendid shelf of a derrière. We have to deal with what we've got, appreciate it and move swiftly on. We all spend far too much time focusing on what we don't have and undermining what we do in the process. It's a cunning little distraction from what is truly important.

In the span of my career and travels I have come across women with extraordinary bodies, who aren't prisoners to frugal eating and self-inflicted misery. These are women who eat sensibly, who might have one day a week featuring some major decadent eating, and exercise in a way that they enjoy, be it boxing, biking, surfing, spinning, yoga, volleyball, gymnastics, pole dancing, running or walking. These women are sexy. They are not necessarily reed-thin or creamily voluptuous. I have met women in the middle and at either end of the spectrum. What they share is a total appreciation for food and eating and an understanding that, whatever their body's shape or size, they are in command. There is a joy about their being.

I have also come across many women who are self-restricted and miserable. There is something deeply joyless in a life consisting of restriction; even in the word itself. Starving is not sexy. It is bleeding gums, acrid breath, brittle bones, osteoporosis, infertility and complication. It saps and withers.

Sexy is inherent in a healthy appreciation for food, in having the energy to romp with your beloved, pick up your baby, cook dinner for your friends, go for a run or simply take a gentle walk to the market. Sexy is in feeling sated, having options and feeling alive.

That damp summer stretched on with great sweetness. I saw my oldest girlfriends and lay laughing on the sofa with them as the rain continued pounding down outside. In July, my family celebrated my little brother Luke's twenty-first birthday; grandmother, mother, aunts, sister, babies and cousins all balanced on the end of the rickety dock in Menemsha, a fishing port in Martha's Vineyard, eating steamed cracked lobster from paper plates with lemon and butter and corn on the cob. We drank ice-cold beer from the bottle and watched the boats sail in.

To everything there is a season; from seventeen to twenty-one, mine was the season of chocolate cake. I didn't know how to eat within the boundaries of reason; instead I learned loudly, through trial and error. In the years that have elapsed since then a lot of groundbreaking work has been done on nutrition and that information is much more widely available. There is also now a general acceptance that factory-farmed meat and dairy products are not good for us, and certainly not good for the animal subjected to all that entails. Jamie Oliver and Hugh Fearnley-Whittingstall have vocally fought the cause on this one, and their steadfastness has created an awareness and change that is marvelous. In a relatively short space of time we have seen dietary trends ebb and flow; low-fat, low-calorie, protein-only, high-fat, low-carb, no-carb *et al*. Hopefully after the initial fuss and flutter we're arriving at a place of good old-fashioned wholesome balance.

As with anything, I don't know all the answers; I'm still learning. That's the fun of it. As I was wrapping this book up I went to stay in a magical hotel in Mexico, near the town of Colima. Hacienda San Antonio is a still, serene place in the mountains. Its name is an homage to Saint Anthony, whom the owner prayed to in the nineteenth century as the rest of the area was being devastated by a volcanic eruption.

"If you save this land that I love," she prayed, "I will build a chapel in your name and this place will be known as your own." The land remained untouched and, as good as her word, she built a chapel and renamed the estate in his name.

I went to Hacienda with my boyfriend after a good few months of solely writing and sticking my nose in and out of the fridge, which as I mentioned before is a big tendency when I'm faced with a computer and left to my own devices. I was feeling a little more ample then usual, and making jokes about declaring my arse at customs as excess baggage.

The food there was exquisite, all sourced either from the working farm and dairy on the estate or as locally as possible. Breakfast was scrambled eggs, with onions, peppers and cheese and delicious natural yogurt with a trail of honey. Lunch was a smorgasbord of whatever you could imagine, but mine tended to be salad, grilled squid, goat's cheese and frittata. The margaritas were epic, and one was had as a ritual at seven o'clock every night, followed by a heaving feast of a dinner; guacamole, fish in a piquant lime coriander sauce, crisp broccoli and carrots from the garden and then a gently wobbling caramelly flan, with thin shavings of hot green peppers dotted in its pale folds.

I ate like this every day for a week, and had some small dessert every day; sometimes twice when faced with something totally delectable at lunchtime, like a soft, springy lemon tart with a crisply burnished crust. Because it is a bit like staying in a house, there isn't really room service or a minibar, so we were eating only at mealtimes. In between we were going for walks, and riding horses through the woods in the afternoon rainy-season rain that fell in sheets for an hour or two and then miraculously stopped, leaving a landscape swollen, green and filled with a clear scent of earth and all that is good.

The moral to this story is that after a week of practicing what I preach, my jeans were loose, my stomach flat, and I left a quarter of my bottom in Mexico.

In the story with a tidy ending, the illness I got in India would have been the ultimate moment of epiphany, but really what happened to me was a series of mini-epiphanies, that I still occasionally have to be reminded of in those unhinged hormonal moments when I feel as if I'm the Michelin man's more corpulent cousin. I now possess a huge sense of humor about both my appetite and affinity for food and I wear it proudly.

I was making jokes about declaring my arse at customs as excess baggage

My unsure baby fat, for that's what it was really, slunk slowly away one year, perhaps to visit another unwitting teenager as an uninvited guest. Its departure left me to my adult self, the only bodily suggestion of adolescence lurking in my battle-scarred knees. The slow joy that my adult self derives from food and cooking is something I cannot imagine being without; it's intrinsic, and devoid of it, life would seem colorless somehow. The thought of it is even balm for insomnia; for when I can't sleep I simply pore through cookery books, which works like a charm. Mrs. Beeton, Delia Smith, M. F. K. Fisher, Nigel Slater, Nigella Lawson, River Cottage books, Jamie Oliver; the list is ever-increasing and my book shelves are buckling.

While writing and testing out this book, I experienced the luxury of ambling through many green markets and specialty food shops on a quest for the ripest peach or the nuttiest piece of pecorino. The wealth of choice was awe-inspiring and I clucked around, happy like an idle hen in the warm grass. This indulgence was doubled in my quiet kitchen as the umpteenth cake slowly baked and Nina Simone sang huskily through the stereo. What struck me, again and again, is that cooking and eating can be so simple, yet both can be a far-reaching expression of love and humanity that is universal. I can hazard a guess that when you recall the memorable moments in your life that revolved around meals you weren't thinking, "And the calorie count was . . ."

For me, wound up in that delicious sense memory bank are so many tiny things: my mother's gooseberry fool, eaten in the garden on a hot still summer night; my father making me scrambled eggs on toast in his kitchen with the checkered

linoleum as his ornery cat Norman watched suspiciously from the sidelines; the smell of my grandmother Gee-Gee's house as she bustled us into the hall; Victoria sponge cake, light as a feather and dripping with homemade raspberry jam, just out of the oven. Waking on the sofa with a flu-filled head as a child, my nanny Maureen there with a bowl of thick lentil soup and a cool hand. The smell of that first charred risotto that I made to impress a boy when I was fifteen; the smell of it working when I made it for my little brother and sister again and again on Sundays. The midnight feast I had in my grandfather's gypsy caravan with my best friend at thirteen, hysterically laughing at the fact that I was now too long for the bunk beds in it, but she at five feet fit them perfectly, and the morning after when my grandfather looked at my squashed, cranky face and roared with laughter as he made us both toast with marmalade. He died that November, and I cherish the memory of that breakfast. Then there is the soup that is made for someone who is grief-stricken; broth that is palatable but lace-thin. The long lazy breakfasts of courtship, when the predominant sense is not of taste but of the heart leaping all over the place, expectant and hopeful. The messy tray composed by a child, with lukewarm tea and burnt bitter toast, presented with heartbreaking gravity, which prompts you to say, "This is the best toast I've ever had in my entire life."

The last supper, conjured after someone has died or left, that you play over again in your head: What did we talk about? What did we eat? How could we not have known that this was going to be it? Grasping the bones of the mundane and holding them close and dear.

I remember a picnic with the boy I love, on the floor of a new house with no furniture and wine in mugs; a birthday dinner cooked with a total salute to the celebrant's taste; the lunch that heralded a labor: these are the things that are rare and precious in all that is higgledy-piggledy and crooked.

Remember this as you cook and eat, and welcome it. And if in the midst of all of it you have time, send me a postcard. Just please don't ask me, "How do I get a six-pack?" Because I will respond as I do now, by saying, "My darling, I have absolutely no clue, nor the inclination to find out."

Happy eating.

summer
breakfasts

Cinnamon roast peaches with vanilla yogurt

Roasting has the same magic culinary effect as soaking. What before might have been a bit withered and cross-looking, under a pat of butter and the oven's fierce gaze becomes full and heavy-bodied with flavor.

Preheat the oven to 450°F. Wash and halve the peaches, removing the pits, and place in a small roasting pan. Sprinkle each peach half with a little cinnamon and brown sugar and dot with the butter or oil. Cook for about 10 minutes.

While the peaches are cooking, mix the yogurt with the vanilla and agave syrup or honey.

Serve the peaches in bowls doused with the yogurt, and garnish with a little fresh mint if you feel fancy.

SERVES 2 GREEDY PEOPLE

4 peaches, ripe but firm
1 teaspoon of ground cinnamon
1 tablespoon of light brown sugar
1 tablespoon of butter or sunflower oil
2 cups of low-fat Greek yogurt
1 teaspoon of vanilla extract
1 tablespoon of agave syrup or honey
Fresh mint leaves (optional)

packed with all things good, with the air of a milkshake

Blueberry strawberry smoothie

SERVES 2

1 cup of frozen
  blueberries
1 cup of frozen
  strawberries
1 scoop of protein
  powder (I use
  Spiru-Tein brand,
  chocolate flavor)
1 cup of unsweetened
  soy milk
Agave syrup or honey
  to taste, if needed
Peanut butter
  (optional)

Packed with all things good, this has the air of a milkshake about it. It is surprisingly filling and will keep you going for hours.

Whack it all in the blender, adding water if you want it slightly thinner. I like smoothies to be thick like milk-shakes. This is also totally divine with a tablespoon of peanut butter added.

Cold frittata with goat's cheese and zucchini

Frittatas are a favorite of mine – you can basically throw anything into them, and they are as delicious cold as they are hot. You can also make them in advance and whisk them onto the table for an *al fresco* lunch.

Slice the zucchini thinly. Heat 1 tablespoon of the olive oil in a pan and cook the slices on a low heat for about 10 minutes. Season them and set aside.

Beat the eggs with a pinch of salt and heat the remaining oil in a small nonstick skillet. Pour in the eggs, zucchini and goat's cheese and cook until lightly browned on the underside. Using a wide spatula, carefully turn over to brown the other side; alternatively, place under a hot broiler for a few minutes. Cut in half and serve at room temperature.

SERVES 2
2 baby zucchini
2 tablespoons of olive oil
Salt and pepper
4 eggs
A handful of goat's cheese, crumbled

Scrambled eggs with watercress and smoked salmon

SERVES 2
1 small bunch of
    watercress
4 eggs
Olive oil
Salt and pepper
4 slices of smoked
    salmon

This reminds me of summer breakfasts at Claridge's Hotel in London. They probably serve it with a lot more aplomb and white linen than I do.

If you'd like to be very Martha Stewart, you can roll the salmon so it stands in a circle and then place the scrambled eggs in the center. . . .

Wash and trim the watercress. Scramble the eggs, not for long, as you know (see page 152), and pour into the salmon rounds or next to the salmon if the thought of making patterns with your food repulses you. You can place the watercress beside the eggs or on top.

Breakfast burrito

SERVES 2

1 tablespoon of olive
  oil
2 scallions, white parts
  only, finely chopped
1 teaspoon of dried red
  chile flakes
½ cup of chopped
  tomatoes
4 eggs
½ cup of cheese –
  Cheddar or similar,
  grated
Salt and pepper
2 tortillas –
  stoneground corn or
  whole wheat
A little chopped fresh
  parsley

I discovered burritos in California and they haven't lost their appeal. As with frittatas, you can fill them with whatever's handy: onions, spinach, goat's cheese . . . the list is endless.

First, heat the olive oil in a pan. Add the scallions, chile and tomatoes and stir for a few minutes. Take off the heat and set aside. Scramble the eggs, adding the cheese at the last minute. Stir in the chiles-tomato mixture and season.

In a nonstick pan, heat the tortillas one after the other, for about 30 seconds each side. Put flat on a plate and spoon on the egg mixture, with the parsley, and roll them up.

Homemade muesli with strawberry yogurt

Muesli is a good staple to have about, and you can add to it as you wish with dried fruits, seeds and grains.

Mix all the dry ingredients well. Stir in the water and leave for an hour (or overnight). Put the yogurt in a blender with the strawberries and 1 teaspoon of honey or agave syrup. Purée. Serve the muesli with a big dollop of yogurt on top.

This cereal can also be cooked with milk or water and eaten hot, like a porridge.

SERVES 2

1 cup of rolled oats
½ cup of spelt flakes
¼ cup of sunflower
  seeds
¼ cup of sliced
  almonds
½ teaspoon of ground
  cinnamon
A small handful of
  dried figs, dried
  apples and raisins,
  finely chopped
1 cup of water
1 cup of plain yogurt
½ cup of ripe
  strawberries
Honey or agave syrup

summer
lunches

Avocado soup

Yet another easy blendery thing. Perhaps this book should be renamed "on a bender with Miss Dahl's blender" . . . maybe not.

Peel the avocados and remove the pits. Into the blender go the apple, avocados, yogurt, chile flakes and lime juice.

Warm the stock to release the flavor. Add the stock to the blender and purée until the soup is a rich, smooth green velvet. Put it in the fridge for a few hours and add some chopped cilantro on top of each bowl when ready to serve.

SERVES 2

2 ripe avocados

1 apple, cored, peeled and sliced into chunks

1 cup of plain yogurt (full-fat works better here)

1 teaspoon of dried red chile flakes

Juice from ½ a lime

2 cups of chicken or vegetable stock

Fresh chopped cilantro, to garnish

Quinoa salad with tahini dressing

SERVES 2

2 cups of vegetable or
chicken broth
1 cup of quinoa
½ a peeled cucumber,
chopped
2 scallions, finely
chopped
1 plum tomato, finely
chopped
1 red bell pepper,
deseeded and finely
chopped
Fresh mint leaves, to
garnish (optional)

For the dressing
¼ cup (or thereabouts)
of olive oil
Juice of 1 lemon
2 tablespoons of tamari
(wheat-free soy sauce)
2 tablespoons of tahini
(sesame seed paste)
½ a clove of garlic,
peeled and chopped
Honey (optional)

The ancient grain again. I could eat tahini on
its own, straight out of the jar. It's also really
good on toast.

Bring the stock to the boil, add the quinoa, cover and
simmer for 10–15 minutes.

Make the dressing – everything in a blender, and you could
maybe add a little honey to taste.

When the quinoa's ready, fluff it, pop the vegetables in,
then douse it with dressing, and perhaps chop a few mint
leaves on top. You probably won't need all of the dressing
but you can keep it in a jar in the fridge for up to a week.

Beet soup

Although it is simplicity personified, beet soup always screams of effort. Maybe it's the color, or the rich ruby earthiness of it. To me, it's Norway in a bowl.

Wash and trim the stalky bits from the beets.

Sweat the scallions in a pan with some olive oil on a low heat until they are translucent. Then add the stock to the scallions and leave on a low heat to warm.

In another pan, cover the beets with water, bring to the boil, then reduce the heat and simmer for about 30 minutes until the beets are tender. Drain, and when cool enough to handle peel off the skins and cut the beets into rough chunks.

Put the beets in a blender with the scallion stock and purée until smooth. Add the shot of vodka, lemon juice and crème fraîche, season and give the mixture another whizz in the blender.

You can serve this hot or cold. Either way, serve with the chopped dill on top, a swirl more of crème fraîche and some chopped hard-boiled egg if you feel like it.

SERVES 4

6 medium-sized beets, washed but not peeled
5 scallions, white parts only
Olive oil
6 cups of vegetable or chicken stock
A shot of vodka
Juice of ½ a lemon
2 tablespoons of crème fraîche, plus extra to serve
Salt and pepper
A good handful of fresh dill, chopped
Chopped hard-boiled egg, to serve (optional)

Pea soup

SERVES 2–4
Olive oil
3 scallions, chopped
3 cups of frozen peas
1 quart of vegetable or
    chicken stock
A good handful of
    fresh mint, chopped,
    plus extra to garnish
Salt and pepper
1 tablespoon of crème
    fraîche

As English as English could be. Reminds me of Wimbledon and lazy afternoons.

In a medium-sized saucepan, heat 1 tablespoon of olive oil and sauté the scallions for about 3 minutes. Add the peas and coat them in the oil, stirring. Add the stock and mint and cook for about 10–15 minutes. Transfer to a blender and whiz – in batches if the blender isn't big enough.

Cool in the fridge, season and whirl in the crème fraîche. Serve with a bit more mint chopped on top.

Summer squash with tomato sauce and pine nuts

This works as a big lunch, and you can also get creative with what you put in or on it. Goat's cheese crumbled on top or some shaved Parmesan would be a happy marriage.

First, make the sauce. Heat a little oil, sweat the onion and garlic for a few minutes, then add the celery and mushrooms. Pour the tomatoes in and simmer on low for about 15 minutes. You could add a pinch of brown sugar and a whistle of salt and pepper – try it.

Grate the summer squash very coarsely. In a nonstick pan, heat a little more oil and throw in the squash and cook on low for about 7 minutes. If it starts to brown you can add a little stock rather than using more oil – you want it to stay its lovely pale yellow color.

Pour it onto a plate and serve as you would spaghetti, with the tomato sauce and the Parmesan, pine nuts and some chopped basil and parsley.

SERVES 2

For the sauce
Olive oil
½ an onion, chopped
1 clove of garlic, peeled
   and chopped
1 celery stalk, chopped
1 cup of chopped
   mushrooms
14½oz can of chopped
   tomatoes, drained
Light brown sugar and
   salt and pepper
   (optional)

1 summer squash,
   peeled
A little vegetable stock
   (optional)
½ cup of grated
   Parmesan
A good handful of
   toasted pine nuts
Chopped fresh basil
   and parsley, to serve

Salad niçoise sans anchovies and potatoes

SERVES 2

2 eggs
1 cup of chopped
    green beans
Crispy romaine lettuce
    – five leaves per
    person, chopped
½ cup of black pitted
    olives
6½oz can of good tuna
    – the Italian kind
    packed in oil

For the dressing
1 scant teaspoon of
    Pommery mustard
½ a clove of garlic,
    peeled and crushed
1 tablespoon of good
    balsamic vinegar
3 tablespoons of
    olive oil

The only purist thing about this salad is my use of canned tuna! I have a love–hate relationship with anchovies. I don't mind their presence – I just don't want to look at them. That's why they're not present here. The potatoes are absent simply because I find them too filling with everything else going on. But put them and the anchovies right back in if it bothers you.

Hard-boil the eggs for about 6 minutes, then drain and plunge into cold water. Peel when cold. Blanch the green beans for 1 minute in boiling water – you want them to be still crunchy.

In a bowl, assemble the lettuce and add to it the olives, the green beans, the hard-boiled eggs, quartered, and the drained tuna. Mix the dressing, and pour over the salad.

Fish cakes

I came up with these because I find breaded fish cakes too heavy in the summer. These are not deep-fried bready, floury fish cakes – instead they are very light and are bound with a bit of mayonnaise rather than breadcrumbs, so they won't make you want to nap for hours after eating them. Unless, of course, you've eaten them with a copious quantity of rosé.

Mix all of the ingredients together except for the egg and oil. Shape the salmon mixture into round patties. Beat the egg and then brush each side of the cakes with it, either using a brush or your fingers.

Heat 1 tablespoon of olive oil in a frying pan and fry the cakes for about 3 minutes on each side, until they are lovely and crispy. Serve with grilled zucchini or a big spinachy salad.

SERVES 2

2 cups of cooked salmon, flaked
1 tablespoon of home-made or good store-bought mayonnaise
1 teaspoon of mustard
A small handful of fresh parsley and dill, chopped
1 egg
1 tablespoon of olive oil

summer suppers

Linguine with tomatoes, lemon, chile and crab

SERVES 2

½ cup of cherry
  tomatoes
Sea salt
1 clove of garlic, peeled
½ a red chile, deseeded
  and finely chopped
3 tablespoons of olive
  oil
Juice and zest of
  1 lemon
¾ cup of cooked fresh
  crabmeat
6oz of whole wheat or
  spelt linguine
Chopped fresh parsley

Stolen, stolen, stolen – this recipe (and variations of) has graced summer menus all over the place, the best and first at the brilliant River Café in London. But oh, it's good and so addictive, and seems to epitomize summer in every bite. If there is one good summer pasta dish in your repertoire this should be it.

Cut the tomatoes into halves and sprinkle them with a little sea salt. In a pestle and mortar, crush the garlic and chile into a red pulp. Mix in the olive oil, lemon juice and zest. Add the crab to the mix if your pestle and mortar is big enough; if not, transfer everything to a slightly bigger bowl.

Cook the pasta so it's *al dente*. Drain, then pour the crab mixture and tomatoes over and sprinkle with parsley. Eat.

Warm ratatouille

SERVES 4

2 eggplants, cubed

2 zucchini, cubed

4 tablespoons or so of
olive oil

2 onions, finely sliced

2 cloves of garlic,
peeled and chopped

½ teaspoon of crushed
coriander seeds

2 red bell peppers,
deseeded and thickly
chopped

4 large tomatoes,
peeled, quartered
and deseeded *or*
a 14½oz can of
peeled tomatoes

Salt and pepper

A huge handful of
fresh cilantro,
chopped

I love the science of ratatouille and the ritual of adding slowly to it. I often find that it's even better the next day after a night in the fridge. I like it with tons of cilantro.

Sprinkle the eggplant and zucchini with a bit of salt, pop them in a colander for an hour or so, then rinse them and pat them dry. Heat 1 tablespoon of oil in a frying pan and brown the vegetables on each side. When this is done, set them aside.

In a big heavy pan or casserole, heat the rest of the oil and add to it the onions, garlic and crushed coriander seeds. Sweat them on low for about 4 minutes. Add the peppers and simmer on low for another 10 minutes. Pour in the tomatoes and keep at low for another 15 minutes. Lastly, add the browned zucchini and eggplant and season.

Serve warm with lashings of chopped cilantro.

Chicken and fennel au gratin

More lovely fennel – serve with a crisp green salad and a glass of Meursault.

Preheat the oven to 375°F. Oil a medium-sized roasting pan with the olive oil, making sure it is evenly coated.

Cook the fennel bulbs whole, in boiling water, for about 5 minutes. Drain, slice into rounds and put on the bottom of the roasting pan. Put the chicken breasts on top and season with salt and pepper. Pour the béchamel over the mixture, sprinkle the Parmesan on top of that and bake until bubbling and golden brown, 30–40 minutes. You can roughly chop some parsley or tarragon and scatter on top to serve.

SERVES 4

Olive oil

2 large fennel bulbs, trimmed and cleaned

4 skinless chicken breasts

Salt and pepper

3 cups of béchamel sauce (see recipe for Cauliflower Cheese, page 118)

½ cup of grated Parmesan

Chopped fresh parsley or tarragon, to serve (optional)

Coconut curry with shrimp

This begs for a garden, tea lights, a balmy night and an Indian summer. Failing that, a candle, friends and a picnic blanket on the kitchen floor.

In a large pan, heat the oil and sweat the onion and garlic for a few minutes. Add the chile and curry powder and cook on low for another few minutes. Add the shrimp and cover with the coconut milk. Cook for 10 minutes. Stir in the lime juice and coconut. Taste and season, and when you are ready to serve, cover with the cilantro.

SERVES 2–3

1 tablespoon of peanut or safflower oil
½ an onion, chopped
1 clove of garlic, peeled and chopped
½ a green chile, deseeded and chopped
1 teaspoon of curry powder
2 cups of peeled raw shrimp
14oz can of light coconut milk
Juice of 3 limes
1 tablespoon of unsweetened shredded coconut
Salt and pepper
A good handful of fresh cilantro, chopped

Grilled vegetables with halloumi cheese

SERVES 2

1 large zucchini
1 medium eggplant
Salt
2 tablespoons of olive
  oil
Juice of ½ a lemon
Ground cumin, for
  dusting
4oz of halloumi cheese,
  thinly sliced

All hail halloumi! I went with my heavily pregnant sister, Clover, to a Greek restaurant in Los Angeles where we had a sizzling frying pan of halloumi placed in front of us. When she went into labor the following day, she called me from the hospital. "You know that cheese?" she said. "Well, I can't stop thinking about it . . ." I understood.

Thinly slice the vegetables lengthwise. Salt the eggplant, leaving it in a colander for 30 minutes or so, then rinse and pat dry.

Preheat the broiler. Mix the olive oil with the lemon juice. Dust the vegetables very lightly with the ground cumin. Pour the olive oil mixture over the vegetables and put under the broiler for a few minutes on each side. As they start to turn a light gold, take them out and put the halloumi on top and then give them another blast until the cheese has softened and turned golden.

Barbecued salmon on a cedar plank

SERVES 4

2lb of tail end salmon
  with skin
Olive oil
Salt and pepper

I adore this because it makes a scene. My aunt Lucy made it when I last visited her in Los Angeles. You can buy cedar planks for the barbecue at most large grocery stores. You'll need a plank about 12 x 6 inches. Cooked this way, the salmon is tender, sweet and smoky; truly a wonder.

First of all, and most important, soak the plank in cold water for 2 hours. Weigh it down so it's completely submerged.

Rub the salmon with olive oil and salt and pepper. Light the grill and, when it's searing hot, wipe the excess water from the cedar plank and place the salmon on it, skin side down. Put it on the grill and close the lid.

The plank will set on fire, but gently – don't be alarmed, this is meant to happen! It should take 10–15 minutes for this to happen. When the whole plank is slightly ablaze, turn the grill off if it's gas or electric; if it's a charcoal one, take the plank off very, very carefully with long barbecue tongs.

Put the flaming plank on a big baking sheet. Serve the salmon with some grilled asparagus, a big salad and some warm new potatoes with olive oil and chives.

Wild rice risotto

I grew up on this, and it became very handy when I stopped eating meat at age eleven. "What shall we feed Sophie?" came the cry. "Oh, just give her some risotto." They did, and I learned how to cook it. This is also very good cold, and you can put it in a greased round mold overnight, refrigerate it and turn it out the next day. It looks splendid.

First, cook the wild rice as directed (double the water to the dry measurement and cook in salted water for 40 minutes). Drain.

In a big pan, heat 2 tablespoons of olive oil and gently sweat the shallots, garlic and leek for about 4 minutes or so. Add the zucchini, carrot and mushrooms and cook for another few minutes. Add the brown rice and stir, making sure it is coated with the oil (add a little extra oil if necessary).

Pour in a little of the warm stock and stir until it has been absorbed by the rice. Give it a quick thimbleful of wine or Pernod. Keep stirring and keep adding stock until the rice is cooked and all the stock has been absorbed – about 35 minutes.

Add the wild rice and with it another spoonful of olive oil. Add the chopped parsley and cilantro and the almonds. Give one last stir and serve.

SERVES 4

½ cup of wild rice
Salt
Olive oil
2 shallots, finely chopped
1 clove of garlic, peeled and crushed
1 leek, white part only, chopped
1 zucchini, coarsely grated
1 carrot, coarsely grated
1 cup of finely sliced wild mushrooms
2 cups of brown rice
6 cups of warm vegetable stock
A slug of white wine or Pernod
A handful each of fresh parsley and cilantro, chopped
½ cup of sliced almonds

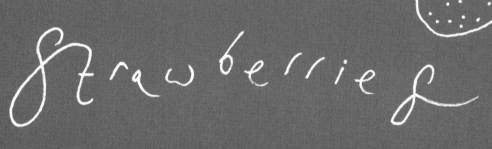

Strawberries

desserts

Ginger parkin
Baked apples
Lemon Capri torte
Lemon mousse
Clover's strawberry pudding
Blackberry and apple crumble
Flourless chocolate cake
Cardamom rice pudding
Elderflower jelly
Flapjacks
Eton mess with rhubarb
Banana bread
Chocolate chestnut soufflé cake
Orange yogurt and polenta cake

Ginger parkin

MAKES 12 SQUARES

2¼ sticks of butter, plus extra for greasing

½ cup of molasses

½ cup of golden syrup

1 cup of light brown sugar

4 cups of flour (I use spelt, as you know, but any flour will do)

2 cups of quick-cook oats

1 teaspoon of baking soda

1 tablespoon of ground ginger

3 eggs, beaten

Parkin (a supermoist gingerbread) is traditionally made and then left alone in an airtight container for between three days and a week in order for it to become deliciously sticky and moist. It's a marvel.

Preheat the oven to 350°F. Grease a 9-inch loaf pan.

In a heavy-bottomed saucepan, melt the butter, molasses, syrup and sugar on a low heat. Keep a vigilant eye, so it doesn't get too hot or burn.

In a big mixing bowl, mix together all the dry ingredients and then gently stir in the warm, treacly buttery mixture until it is thoroughly mixed in with the dry. Add the beaten eggs. Pour into the pan and bake for around 45 minutes.

When you take it out, let it cool and then transfer into your airtight container. Do not break it apart! Leave it for at least three days, and then serve it in all its moist mysterious glory, feeling smug.

Baked apples

You can sort of do whatever you want with baked apples – including making them as decadent or frugal as you wish. Here is a semidecadent version.

Preheat the oven to 350°F.

Wash and core the apples, leaving about an inch at the bottom intact so they are not hollow throughout. Mix together the butter, sugar, raisins, walnuts and cinnamon. Stuff the apples with the mixture. Place them in a roasting tray with a few inches of hot water covering the bottom and bake for 40 minutes.

Serve with anything from yogurt to mascarpone to thick vanilla ice cream.

SERVES 4

4 big cooking apples
1 tablespoon of butter
¼ cup of light brown
  sugar
¼ cup of raisins
¼ cup of chopped
  walnuts
1 teaspoon of ground
  cinnamon

as decadent or frugal as you wish

Lemon Capri torte

SERVES 6

1½ sticks of butter,
  plus extra for
  greasing
1 cup of superfine
  sugar
6 eggs, separated
Zest and juice of
  4 lemons
2 cups of blanched
  almonds, toasted,
  then ground
1 cup of potato flour,
  plus extra for
  flouring the pan

I got this recipe from a taxi driver in Sorrento, who was big on cooking. He said his wife and daughters begged him not to, though, because he left the kitchen in such a mess!

Preheat the oven to 400°F. Grease and flour a 9-inch round cake pan. (I prefer to use a springform pan.)

Cream the butter and sugar, add the egg yolks in one go, then add the lemon zest and lemon juice. In a separate bowl, whisk the egg whites until they form soft peaks and add to the mixture. Last, fold in the ground almonds and flour. Pour the mixture into the cake pan and bake in the oven for 10 minutes, then turn the oven down to 300°F and cook for another 40 minutes. Cool and invert the cake onto a serving plate. You can get creative with this; I was disgusting and iced it with a mixture of crème fraîche and lemon curd!

Lemon mousse

SERVES 4

1½ teaspoons of
   unflavored gelatin
Juice of 3 lemons
3 large eggs, separated
¾ cup of superfine
   sugar
Grated zest of 1 lemon
1 pinch of salt
1 cup of heavy cream
A handful of fresh
   mint, chopped

When I was a little girl this was the Sunday standard request. I use the recipe handed down to me featured in my grandfather and step-grandmother's cookbook, *Memories with Food at Gipsy House*.

Dissolve the gelatin with the lemon juice in a bowl over simmering water. Beat the egg yolks with half the sugar until they are ribbony. Fold the gelatin mixture and the lemon zest into the yolk mixture. Beat the egg whites with a pinch of salt to soft peak stage. Add the remaining sugar and beat back into soft peaks. In another bowl, whip the cream until very stiff.

Fold 1 tablespoon of the egg whites into the almost-set lemon mixture, then fold in the cream and remaining egg whites. Pour into four ramekins or one big dish and put in the fridge for several hours. Cover with chopped mint and serve.

Clover's strawberry pudding

In England, this would be called milk jelly. Either way, it reminds me of everything good about being little, including my sister Clover, who devoured bowlfuls. I'm hoping this dessert gene passes on to my nephew Finley so we can call it tradition. Children love it.

Dissolve the gelatin in the hot water. When the mixture is cool, whisk in the evaporated milk until the mixture is thick and frothy. Leave it to set for at least 2 hours. Cover with strawberry slices, swirls of cream and curls of grated chocolate, if you wish – the flashier the better, really.

SERVES 4

1 packet of gelatin – strawberry is particularly good
½ cup of hot water
12oz can of evaporated milk
Slices of strawberry, swirls of cream and curls of grated chocolate, to decorate (optional)

Blackberry and apple crumble

Everyone should know how to make a crumble – an old faithful and very difficult to get wrong. It delivers that lovely nursery feeling of a comforting inner spoonful. You can substitute any number of ingredients for the fruit filling, such as raspberries, rhubarb, black cherries, blueberries, apricots – even a prune and Armagnac version if you're feeling adventurous.

Preheat the oven to 400°F.

You can mix the flour, oats and the 1 stick of butter in a food processor, or you can do it with your fingers in a mixing bowl. You want it to look like nubbly breadcrumbs. Either way, when it has reached this texture, mix in the brown sugar. Put your blackberries and apples into a pie dish and dot them with the 1 tablespoon of butter and the sugar. Cover the fruit with the crumble and bake it in the oven for about 30 minutes until the fruit is bubbling up and the crumble is a rich golden brown.

Serve with custard or crème fraîche.

SERVES 6

1 cup of flour of your choice (I use spelt)
½ cup of rolled oats
1 stick of butter, plus 1 tablespoon for the fruit
¼ cup of light brown sugar, plus 2 tablespoons for covering the fruit
8oz of blackberries (fresh or frozen)
8oz of apples, cored and chopped

Flourless chocolate cake

Butter for greasing
2 cups of broken
  semisweet chocolate
  (or 1 cup each of
  dark and milk
  chocolate), plus extra
  to decorate (optional)
1 cup of superfine
  sugar
¾ cup of boiling water
2 sticks of salted
  butter, cut into cubes
6 eggs, separated
1 teaspoon of instant
  coffee
1 tablespoon of vanilla
  extract

To top the cake
1 cup of raspberries,
  whole
1 cup of strawberries,
  quartered
7oz tub of crème
  fraîche

This is the mother of all chocolate cakes. It is incredibly rich and very good cold from the fridge, smothered in crème fraîche. Eat it at your discretion. I dedicate this with love to Ben, a fellow chocolate fiend.

Grease and line the base of an 8-inch square or 9-inch round cake pan (though I prefer to use a springform pan as the texture of the cake is quite moist and sticky). Preheat the oven to 350°F.

In a large food processor (or do in two batches), pulse the chocolate and sugar until fine. Add the boiling water, butter, egg yolks, coffee and vanilla extract. In a glass bowl, whisk the egg whites until stiff and then add them to the mixture in the food processor and blend for 10 seconds or so. Pour the mixture into the prepared cake pan and put in the hot oven for 45–55 minutes. The top will be cracked like a desert fault line.

After you take the cake out of the oven it will collapse in on itself quite a bit. This is OK; it's not meant to be a proud cool cake, it's meant to look slightly rough around the edges and homemade, and the crème fraîche and berries will hide any dips and cracks!

Let the cake cool, then put it in the fridge for a few hours. When you are ready to serve, remove from the pan and smother it in raspberries, strawberries and crème fraîche. You can also grate some more chocolate on top.

My favorite, favorite thing!

Cardamom rice pudding

SERVES 6–8

5½ cups of the milk of
   your choice – I use
   2%
1 cinnamon stick
1½ cups of basmati
   rice
1 tablespoon of vanilla
   extract
8 cardamom pods
½ cup of superfine
   sugar or ½ cup of
   maple syrup
½ cup of raisins
½ cup of sliced
   almonds

I adore rice pudding. This one is a bit like a risotto in that it takes a little while, but it is still incredibly easy. I like it both hot and cold – cold it's delicious with a teaspoon of strawberry jam.

Pour the milk into a big heavy-bottomed pan with the cinnamon stick. Bring it to the boil and stir in the rice and vanilla extract. Simmer on a very low heat for about 30 minutes, making sure that you keep stirring so the rice does not stick to the pan.

In a pestle and mortar, crush the cardamom pods and extract their seeds. Throw the pods away and add the crushed seeds to the sugar. (If you are using maple syrup instead of sugar, add the seeds separately to the rice pan now.) When the rice looks like a soupy milky risotto, stir in the raisins, almonds and cardamom sugar or maple syrup, and cook for another 5–10 minutes on low, adding more milk if it starts to get dry.

Elderflower jelly

Blissfully easy, and perfect to eat on a summer night in the garden.

Make the jelly base by mixing your gelatin with the hot water. Make up the elderflower cordial separately, with about 10 tablespoons to 2 cups of cold water, making sure it is strong – add more cordial if necessary. Stir the gelatin mixture into the cordial and pour into a serving bowl or a pretty mold. Let it set in the fridge for at least 2 hours and serve with a blob of whipped cream and/or a shortbread biscuit.

SERVES 4

1 packet of unflavored gelatin
½ cup of hot water
½ cup plus 2 tablespoons of elderflower cordial
2 cups of cold water

perfect to eat on a
summer night in the garden

Flapjacks

**MAKES 12
SQUARES**
Butter for greasing
½ cup of honey
1 tablespoon of
   molasses
1½ sticks of butter
1¾ cups of rolled oats
1 teaspoon of vanilla
   extract

Flapjacks mean bonfire nights, smoky evenings
and children's parties. Or another one of those
individual pleasures, eaten while nestling on
the sofa with your favorite book, sticky-
fingered. Or they work equally well served to a
prim gathering when you're trying to score
domestic brownie points.

Preheat the oven to 350°F. Grease a large rimmed baking
sheet.

In a heavy-bottomed saucepan, on a low heat, heat the
honey, molasses and butter, until the butter has melted.
Remove from the heat, stir in the oats and vanilla and press
the mixture firmly into the baking sheet. Bake for 25–30
minutes until golden. Leave to cool briefly, then cut in
squares while still a little warm. Store in an airtight
container.

Eton mess with rhubarb

Eton mess is such a quintessentially English summer dessert. For me it sums up lazy cricket matches, roses in full bloom and the sharp tang of rhubarb on the tip of your tongue. Its biggest joy is that it's one massive, delightful, creamy mess, and it doesn't pretend to be anything else.

First, make the meringues. Preheat the oven to 275°F. Line a large cookie sheet with nonstick parchment paper. In a very clean bowl, whisk the egg whites until they reach firm peaks. Gradually mix in the sugar and salt and whisk well until the mixture is a thick spool of white. This should take about 8 minutes and obviously an electric mixer would be a little bit of a blessing here.

Spoon the mixture into blobs on your cookie sheet, leaving a generous gap between them. Bake for 1 hour.

While the meringue is baking, make the rhubarb compote. In a pan, boil the water with the sugar and add the rhubarb when it starts bubbling. Stir and let it cook for about 5 minutes. When the rhubarb is tender, remove from the heat. Add the rose water and set aside.

Now for the mess bit. You can either do this in six pretty glasses or one big bowl. Whip the cream until soft and fluffy. Add to it the rhubarb and mash it in with the meringues. You can do this with some order in layers, or in a happy haphazard fashion; either way it's totally delicious. Serve with some toasted almond slivers if you like.

NOTE:
This quantity of mixture makes 36 small meringues, so you can keep the extras in an airtight tin.

SERVES 6

For the meringues
6 large egg whites
1½ cups of superfine sugar
1 pinch of salt
Toasted almond slivers, to serve (optional)

For the compote
½ cup of boiling water
3 tablespoons of superfine sugar
1lb of rhubarb, chopped
1 teaspoon of rose water
2 cups of heavy cream

Banana bread

SERVES 6
5⅓ tablespoons of soft
   butter, plus extra for
   greasing and serving
4 ripe bananas,
   mashed up
1 cup of light brown
   sugar
1 egg, beaten
1 tablespoon of vanilla
   extract
1 teaspoon of baking
   soda
1 pinch of salt
1½ cups of flour (spelt
   or whatever)

I used to make banana bread in the fierce
winters when I lived in New York and it was too
freezing to do anything but bake. Eat it warm
out of the oven with a lick of butter – it's
unadulterated manna.

Preheat the oven to 350°F. Grease a 9 x 5-inch pan.

Pour the mashed bananas into a big mixing bowl. Mix in
the butter, sugar, egg and vanilla extract. Add the baking
soda and salt and mix in the flour last. Pour into the
prepared pan. Bake for 1 hour, remove and cool, then serve
in slices with a little butter.

Chocolate chestnut soufflé cake

SERVES 6

Butter for greasing

4oz semisweet or dark chocolate, chopped small

½ cup of unsweetened cocoa powder

¾ cup of superfine sugar

½ cup of boiling water

½ cup of chestnut purée

2 egg yolks

½ cup of spelt flour

1 tablespoon of rum

1 teaspoon of vanilla extract

4 egg whites

¼ teaspoon of cream of tartar

½ teaspoon of lemon juice

This is a very grown-up cake. The combination of rum and chestnuts makes it a dark, decadent pleasure. Perfect for an adult occasion!

Preheat the oven to 350°F. Grease and line the base of a 9-inch springform pan with parchment paper.

In a large bowl, combine the chocolate, cocoa powder and half the sugar. Slowly pour in the boiling water and whisk until smooth. Stir in the chestnut purée, egg yolks, spelt flour, rum and vanilla extract and set aside.

In another bowl, combine the egg whites with the cream of tartar and the lemon juice. Beat at medium speed until soft peaks form. Gently pour in the remaining sugar, beating continuously at a high speed now, until the egg whites are stiff. Fold a quarter of this mixture into the chocolate mixture until it melds. Then fold the rest in.

Pour the mixture into the cake pan. Bake for 35 minutes – don't be tempted to open the oven before the time's up. Serve with some cold vanilla custard.

Orange yogurt and polenta cake

Another summery one.

Preheat the oven to 350°F and grease and line the base of a 9-inch cake pan with parchment paper.

Cream the butter and sugar together and whisk in the eggs, one at a time. In a separate bowl, mix the flours together and then add them to the egg-and-sugar mixture. Whisk in the polenta, almonds, Greek yogurt, honey, orange juice and orange zest. Pour into the prepared cake pan and bake for 45–60 minutes. Check after 45 minutes by inserting a skewer into the center of the cake. If it comes out clean, the cake is done. If not, cook for a few minutes longer.

You can make a lemon-sugar syrup to drizzle it with – but I like it on its own.

Lemon drizzle

Put ½ cup of superfine sugar into a bowl and stir in 3 tablespoons of lemon juice. Pour over the cake when it comes out of the oven.

1 stick of butter, plus extra for greasing
1 cup of superfine sugar
3 eggs
½ cup of spelt flour
½ cup of self-rising flour
¾ cup of polenta
½ cup of ground almonds
⅓ cup of full-fat Greek yogurt
2 tablespoons of honey
¼ cup of orange juice
Finely grated zest of 2 oranges

acknowledgments

Thank you first and foremost to my lovely Jamie for cooking and eating with the same passion as me, and for being such a star among men.

Thank you to my entire family for meeting my greed with such celebration and joining in it over the years: Mummy, Daddy, Maureen, Clover, Luke and Ned and the Tantes. Thank you to my other family, the heavenly Cullums: John, Yvonne and Ben, for getting it, even if you don't eat as much as other families . . .

Huge thanks to all the people who endlessly talked with me about food, humored me and shared their recipes and techniques with me, in particular the gorgeous Carissa Perret, Lauren Hampson and Tiffany Crouch.

Thank you again, Liccy Dahl, for opening your kitchen and arms to me and letting me raid your larder on a regular basis.

Thank you, thank you, Jan Baldwin, for your breathtaking photographs and instinct, and thank you, Patrick Budge, for your beautiful design and layouts. Thank you, Susie Theodorou, for being far more organized than I could ever be and making everything in your path delectable.

My thanks also to Jan's capable team: Peter Dixon, Wayne Kirk, Jonny Birch, Shannon Doohan and Helen Carter; and to Susie's meticulous assistants Rebecca Jurkevich, Laura Fyfe and Sammie Bell.

Thank you, Grainne Fox, for your sage calm, support and keen eye.

Thank you, Ed Victor, Maggie Phillips and Linda Van, for beginning the journey with me.

A massive thank-you and hug to everyone at HarperCollins who have patiently made this book such a source of pride: Belinda Budge, Carole Tonkinson, Katy Carrington, Lee Motley and Anna Valentine.

Thank you to my erstwhile stable of girlfriends, for providing laughter, sense and sweetness while eating chocolate cake on the sofa long into the night.

And lastly, welcome, little Finley Fiandaca – my darling nephew. I only hope you like eating as much as the rest of us!

With love and thanks to all of you,

index

acorn squash, my mama's baked 162

agave syrup 142
grilled bananas with Greek yogurt and agave 92

alcohol 144

Allen, Darina 77

apples
baked apples 245, **246, 247**
blackberry and apple crumble **254**, 255

apricots
oatmeal with apricots, manuka honey and crème fraîche 90

artichokes
char-grilled artichoke hearts with Parmesan and winter greens 103

asparagus
asparagus soup with Parmesan 168–9
fava bean salad with pecorino and asparagus 172, **173**

avocado
avocado soup **218**, 219
shrimp, avocado, grapefruit, watercress and pecan salad **190**, 191

baby vegetable fricassee 171

baked apples 245, **246, 247**

baked eggs with Swiss chard 40, **41**

baked haddock ramekin 31

bananas
banana bread 266, **267**
grilled bananas with Greek yogurt and agave 92

barbecued salmon on a cedar plank 240

béchamel sauce 118

beet soup 221, **222–3**

black olive salsa 178

blackberry and apple crumble **254**, 255

Blow, Isabella 3–5, 12

blueberry strawberry smoothie 208

bread
banana bread 266, **267**
homemade 28
wholesome 144

breakfast burrito **212, 213**, 214

brown rice risotto with pumpkin, mascarpone, sage and almonds 111

buckwheat risotto with wild mushrooms 48, **49**

buttermilk chicken with smashed sweet potatoes 119

butternut squash
spelt pancakes filled with cream cheese and butternut squash 99

caravan **x**, 24, 200, 201

cardamom rice pudding 258

carrots, for Sunday roast 55

cauliflower cheese 118

celeriac
celeriac and parsnip purée 54–5
fish pie with celeriac mash 116, **117**

char-grilled artichoke hearts with Parmesan and winter greens 103

char-grilled scallops on pea purée 185

chestnut and mushroom soup 107

chicken
buttermilk chicken with smashed sweet potatoes 119
chicken and fennel au gratin 235
chicken and halloumi kebabs with chanterelles 44
chicken soup with chickpeas 98
chicken stew with green olives 188, **189**
my dad's chicken curry 112, **113**
Sunday roast chicken and trimmings 54–5

chocolate
chocolate chestnut soufflé cake 268
flourless chocolate cake 256

Christmas 122–7

cilantro dressing 39

cinnamon roast peaches with vanilla yogurt **204**, 205

Clover (sister) 145, 238

Clover's strawberry pudding 251, **252, 253**

coconut curry with shrimp **236**, 237

cold frittata with goat's cheese and zucchini 209

coquette's eggs 152

cornbread stuffing 124

crab
crab and fennel salad 163, **165**
linguine with tomatoes, lemon, chile and crab 232

crusted rack of lamb for Luke **182, 183**, 184

Dahl, Roald (grandfather) 92, 201, 250
Dahl, Tessa (mother) 3, 7, 9, 65, 73, 145, 162, 166, 199
Doukas, Sarah 12

eggplant
  eggplant Parmigiana 63
eggs
  baked eggs with Swiss chard 40, **41**
  coquette's eggs 152
  hangover eggs 91
  omelette with caramelized red onion and Red Leicester 22, **23**
  poached eggs on portobello mushrooms with goat's cheese 18, **19**
  scrambled eggs with red chiles and vine tomatoes 86
  scrambled eggs with watercress and smoked salmon 210, **211**
elderflower jelly 259, **260, 261**
Eton mess with rhubarb 263, **264, 265**

fava bean salad with pecorino and asparagus 172, **173**
Fearnley-Whittingstall, Hugh 197
fennel
  chicken and fennel au gratin 235
  crab and fennel salad 163, **165**
Ferré, Gianfranco 13
figs, grilled with ricotta and thyme honey 156, **157**
fish cakes **228, 229**
fish pie with celeriac mash 116, **117**
fish soup, Hortense's **180**, 181
flapjacks 262

flourless chocolate cake 256
French onion soup 35, **37**

Gee-Gee (grandmother) 71–3, 86, 201
ginger parkin 244
goat's cheese
  cold frittata with goat's cheese and zucchini 209
  poached eggs on portobello mushrooms with goat's cheese 18, **19**
  spinach and watercress salad with goat's cheese 34
grilled bananas with Greek yogurt and agave 92
grilled figs with ricotta and thyme honey 156, **157**
grilled papaya with lime **148**, 149
grilled salmon with baked onions **64**, 65
grilled vegetables with halloumi cheese 238, **239**

haddock
  baked haddock ramekin 31
halibut
  pan-fried orange halibut with watercress purée 179
halloumi cheese
  chicken and halloumi kebabs with chanterelles 44
  grilled vegetables with halloumi cheese 238, **239**
hangover eggs 91
hidden sugar 143
Hollers' curried parsnip soup 102
Holloway, Julian (father) 102, 112, 199–201
homemade muesli with strawberry yogurt 215
Hortense's fish soup **180**, 181

Indian sweet potato pancakes 30

kedgeree with brown rice 85
Knight, Nick 13

La Chapelle, David 13
Lagerfeld, Karl 13
lamb
  crusted rack of lamb for Luke **182, 183**, 184
lemon and ricotta spelt pancakes 155
lemon Capri torte 248, **249**
lemon mousse 250
lettuce soup, Teddy's 166
Lily's stir-fry with tofu 59, **60**
linguine with tomatoes, lemon, chile and crab 232
low-calorie/low-fat myth 143
Lucy (aunt) 69, 74, 240
Luke (brother) 140, 145, 156, 184, 197

manuka honey
  oatmeal with apricots, manuka honey and crème fraîche 90
Maureen (nanny) 5, 47, 201
McGrath, Pat 135
Meisel, Steven 135, 136
monkfish with saffron sauce **114**, 115
Morris, Annie 56
Moss, Kate 12, 135
mushrooms
  buckwheat risotto with wild mushrooms 48, **49**
  chestnut and mushroom soup 107
  chicken and halloumi kebabs with chanterelles 44
  poached eggs on portobello mushrooms with goat's cheese 18, **19**

scrambled tofu with cumin and shiitake mushrooms 84

sea bass in tarragon and wild mushroom sauce 58

musician's breakfast 28

my dad's chicken curry 112, **113**

my mama's baked acorn squash 162

Ned (brother) 22

oatmeal with apricots, manuka honey and crème fraîche 90

Oliver, Jamie 7, 197, 199

omelette with caramelized red onion and Red Leicester 22, **23**

onions
French onion soup 35, **37**
grilled salmon with baked onions **64**, 65
omelette with caramelized red onion and Red Leicester 22, **23**

orange yogurt and polenta cake 269

pan-fried orange halibut with watercress purée 179

papaya, grilled with lime **148**, 149

Paris mash 56, **57**

parsnips
celeriac and parsnip purée 54–5
Hollers' curried parsnip soup 102

peaches
cinnamon roast peaches with vanilla yogurt **204**, 205

pears
pear and ginger muffins **82**, 83

rice pudding with pear purée 21

peas
char-grilled scallops on pea purée 185
pea soup 224

peasant soup 52

pecorino
fava bean salad with pecorino and asparagus 172, **173**

peppers
squid salad with char-grilled peppers and cilantro dressing **38**, 39

pesto 154

poached eggs on portobello mushrooms with goat's cheese 18, **19**

pumpkin
brown rice risotto with pumpkin, mascarpone, sage and almonds 111

quinoa
quinoa salad with tahini dressing 220
turmeric tofu with cherry tomato quinoa pilaf 187

ratatouille, warm 234

red cabbage, Christmas 125

rhubarb
Eton mess with rhubarb 263, **264**, **265**
rhubarb compote with orange-flower yogurt and pistachios 159

rice pudding, cardamom 258

rice pudding cereal with pear purée 21

ricotta
grilled figs with ricotta and thyme honey 156, **157**
lemon and ricotta spelt pancakes 155

salmon
barbequed salmon on a cedar plank 240
fish cakes **228**, 229
grilled salmon with baked onions **64**, 65
scrambled eggs with watercress and smoked salmon 210, **211**

scallops, char-grilled on pea purée 185

scrambled eggs with red chiles and vine tomatoes 86

scrambled eggs with watercress and smoked salmon 210, **211**

scrambled tofu with cumin and shiitake mushrooms 84

scrambled tofu with pesto and spinach 154

sea bass
sea bass in tarragon and wild mushroom sauce 58
sea bass with black olive salsa and baby zucchini **177**, 178

shrimps
coconut curry with shrimp **236**, 237
shrimp, avocado, grapefruit, watercress and pecan salad **190**, 191

spelt pancakes filled with cream cheese and butternut squash 99

spinach
spinach and watercress salad with goat's cheese 34
spinach barley soup 47
scrambled tofu with pesto and spinach 154

squid salad with char-grilled peppers and cilantro dressing **38**, 39

strawberries
  blueberry strawberry
    smoothie 208
  homemade muesli with
    strawberry yogurt 215
summer squash with
  tomato sauce and pine
  nuts 225
Sunday roast chicken and
  trimmings 54–5
sweet cravings 144
sweet potatoes
  buttermilk chicken with
    smashed sweet potatoes
    119
  Indian sweet potato
    pancakes 30
  roasted with rosemary **182**,
    184
Swiss chard, baked eggs with
  40, **41**
Swiss muesli 153

tahini dressing 220
tawny granola 25
Teddy's lettuce soup 166
tofu
  Lily's stir-fry with tofu 59,
    60
  scrambled tofu with cumin
    and shiitake mushrooms
    84

scrambled tofu with pesto
  and spinach 154
turmeric tofu with cherry
  tomato quinoa pilaf 187
tomatoes
  linguine with tomatoes,
    lemon, chile and crab 232
  scrambled eggs with red
    chiles and vine tomatoes
    86
  summer squash with
    tomato sauce and pine
    nuts 225
  turmeric tofu with cherry
    tomato quinoa pilaf 187
turkey 122–3, **126**, 127
turmeric tofu with cherry
  tomato quinoa pilaf 187
turnip and rutabaga purée
  125

Walker, Tim 135
warm ratatouille 234
warm winter vegetable salad
  96, **97**
watercress
  pan-fried orange halibut
    with watercress purée 179
  scrambled eggs with
    watercress and smoked
    salmon 210, **211**
  shrimp, avocado, grapefruit,

watercress and pecan
  salad **190**, 191
spinach and watercress
  salad with goat's cheese
  34
zucchini and watercress
  soup 179
wild rice risotto 241
winter fruit compote **88**, 89

yogurt
  cinnamon roast peaches
    with vanilla yogurt **204**,
    205
  grilled bananas with Greek
    yogurt and agave 92
  homemade muesli with
    strawberry yogurt 215
  orange yogurt and polenta
    cake 269
  rhubarb compote with
    orange-flower yogurt and
    pistachios 159

zucchini
  cold frittata with goat's
    cheese and zucchini 209
  sea bass with black olive
    salsa and baby zucchini
    177, 178
  zucchini and watercress
    soup 179

suppliers

Crockery: Brickett Davda bowls and plates, www.brickettdavda.com; Jasper Conran for
    Wedgwood, www.wedgwood.com
Olive wood chopping boards: www.andreabrugi.com
Asian-style bowls: www.kriscoad.com
Ceramic lanterns: Jacqui Roche Product Design, www.greatwesternstudios.com,
    jroche2005@yahoo.co.uk
Linens: Society, www.societylimonta.com, available from Mint, www.mintshop.co.uk
Wallpapers: (endpapers/page 2 "Firework Flower," page 68 "Currant Leaf") courtesy of
    Neisha Crosland, www.neishacrosland.com; (pages 130, 194) courtesy of Second Hand
    Rose (New York, USA), www.secondhandrose.com